How to Find Yourself
(or a reasonable facsimile)

The Head-Book Handbook

by

Vincent Eaton

Forward by
Doctor Louis Templeton-Arf, MD, PhD, fiddle-de-de

hidden people

Copyright © 2009, 2010 by Vincent Eaton.

All rights reserved. The moral rights of the author have been asserted.

ISBN 978-0-9561208-0-9

No part of this book may be posted on-line without prior permission of the publisher.

For information, email all inquiries to: hi@hidden-people.net

Published by Hidden People

hidden people

www.hidden-people.net

Second edition

Book design by www.fontana-design.com

Follow the author online at www.vincenteaton.com

How to Find Yourself
(or a reasonable facsimile)

A thin book on a large subject

This book is a compilation of scientific studies and expert opinion addressing practical methods and current theories in Finding Yourself. The casual reader will find illuminating case histories, pure psychobabble conjecture, alternative viewpoints, dreamy reminisces, cheap-shot journalistic reporting and some things that just popped up and sounded halfway reasonable. The professional reader won't give this a second glance.

    The aim of this book is to supply readers with practical examples and helpful hints as to how to spot, understand, and instill a real sense of self in your innermost being. This book's contents should guide readers to a more practical self-knowledge, peace of mind, spiritual nurturing, fuzzy thinking, and strange sexual longings you really should just keep to yourself.

This book is dedicated to all those people
who have misplaced themselves temporarily.

Contents

Foreword: Dr. Louis Templeton-Arf	1
Introduction	5
A Partial Checklist of where not to Find Yourself	7
History and Self	9
The False-Self-Actualization Syndrome: Case Study	13
The Moral Dilemma of Finding Yourself	19
How to Find Yourself during Adolescence	23
The Role of the Anatomy in the Search for Self	25
Business and Identity: Case Study	31
The Subconscious versus the Unconscious in the Search for Self Maggie Debrie, Syndicated Columnist	37
Onanistic Bliss as a Path to the Soul	47
How to Do Introspection Sir Roger Thornsworth III	55
How to Find Yourself through (or in spite of) Marriage: Case Study	61
The Importance of Focus	69
The Implosion Theory Dr. Maxwell P. Appleberry, PhD	73
Warning: The Dangers of Not Finding Yourself	81
Finding Your Own Voice	87

Madness and a Sense of Self: Case Study	89
Schizophrenia and You	99
Inner Peace and a Sense of Self	101
How to Buy Yourself	107
The First Annual Convention of Certified Madmen and Weird People: An Eye Witness Report	111
Further Reading	119
Glossary	121
Endnote	125
Acknowledgments	127
About the Author	129

Foreword
Doctor Louis Templeton-Arf,
MD, PhD, fiddle-de-de

Dr. Templeton-Arf[1] is the world-renown author of those milestone tomes on existence and life: Why?, Volumes I and II, as well as the companion volumes, Because!, Volumes I, II, III, IV, V and VI.

I find, as I sit down to write this forward, that I am in the midst of an Historical Occasion, even though it is sunny outside, the 3rd of May, with Spring in the air and birds singing their familiar territorial songs just outside my window, which gives me a bit of a headache, brought on partly by my wife who is in one of her moods again, compounded by the death of my dog last night. Mysterious causes. Anyway, an Historical Occasion it is, because, with the publication of this well-documented, thoroughly researched volume on the eternal search for self-knowledge—of which contemporary society is but an aberrant manifestation—a long, traumatic era of human

---

[1] Dr. Templeton-Arf is a Visiting Fellow from Oxford, England. At other times, he's a nice guy or a real understanding person. Most of the time, however, he's just a Visiting Fellow.

history may come to an end, just like my dog, Peppy.

Of late, Civilized Men and Women, who have far too much money and free time on their hands, have decided, in alarming numbers, to notice their navels, and, *en masse*, begin murmuring soothing metaphysical terms at these innocent, blank-eyed belly buttons. Without proper supervision.

While I had believed that the subject had been exhausted, that the bottomless pit of the individual navel gazer had been done to death, just like Peppy, now here arrives *How to Find Yourself* to show that previous literature had only scratched the surface of the belly button phenomenon. The book you now hold in your hands plumbs the depths of unadulterated self-absorption and beyond. Way beyond. Beyond any real need or rational justification. Nevertheless ... nice word, nevertheless ... here it is, glistening between its magnificence covers, ready for unsuspecting minds to devour, digest, comprehend, grow depressed, whither away.

However, it's not as bad as all that, although the ache in my back is killing me, and my bowel movements, well, they've not been quite as regular as a gastrointestinal specialist would desire, though things could be worse, oh yes, much, much worse. Just think of Peppy.

In conclusion, I believe it is my primary duty to put forth one emphatic warning:

Watch out!

This book may change your life! It is that powerful, that challenging, that potentially overwhelming.

However, if you find it does not change your life, I would suggest you read it a second time and try harder.

Now, I entreat you to begin your own personal journey into

(or a reasonable facsimile)

this Historical Occasion. Please, turn the page, take a breath, and dive in.

Meanwhile, I shall halt the writing this Foreword, before it goes on and on ... and on ... risking becoming a Backword.

Oh Peppy, where are you?

Introduction

First things first.
    Who am I?
    Go on, say it, say it to yourself.
    "Who am I?"
    Say it aloud:
    "Who am I?"
    Yes, indeed, who *are* you?
    This is the essential question that faces the vast majority of thinking peoples living in these disturbing times. Yet before you begin this book, you must face a stark reality that:
    There has been a great, great deal of mischief caused in the name of self-knowledge.
    Quiet normal brains that would have made fine pharmacists, capable secretaries, or so-so amateur actors take total leave of their senses when deciding to come to grips with identity crises, personality conflicts, feelings of existential anguish, the alarming memories of toilet training, not to mention dealing with the red red robin when it comes bob-bob-bobbing along. These days, many people have been trying to find themselves yet haven't the faintest

idea how to.

The reader should recognize that just as there have been only a few individuals who could do certain tasks really well—natural geniuses in gardening, overpaid handymen, or those teaching sign language to chimpanzees and actually getting paid for it—so too has there been only a select number of beings who have had sufficient education, wisdom, and grounding to find themselves, and not make a complete mess of it.

Nevertheless, certain economically advantaged groups persist in wanting to have a go at finding out who they really are, and the consequences be damned.

To exploit this market need, this book has been thrown together over the last fifteen years for the express purpose of enabling your average self-seeker to discover those meaningful parts of his or her being that vaguely resemble his or her own Self.

Consuming the facts and stories in this book does not demand any specialized educational background, you don't have to tell us who your parents are, we *don't want to know* how they treated you, and best of all you won't be required to take any tests to see whether you have passed or failed after finishing the book. You'll just *be*, at last.

So good luck, whoever you are, whoever you are about to become. So begin your journey into your darkest, most innermost self (flashlight and batteries not included).

A Partial Checklist of where not to Find Yourself

First of all, do not look underneath the living room couch.

Avoid excessive navel-gazing. You will usually not be there, either. Contrary to popular belief, navel-gazing has been determined by the vast majority of mental health experts to be a purely theoretical rather than practical aid in Finding Oneself.

Do not travel to foreign countries with the express purpose to discover who you are. For instance, if you live in North America, never use the commonly heard declaration, "I'm going to Europe to find myself." Often, you will not be there.

Attending purely religious ceremonies should be actively shunned when trying to Find Yourself. Supreme Beings and Blind Faith are generally considered distractions where massive self-absorption is required.

Avoid strenuous nose blowing. Recent medical studies have shown that overexertion of the sinus cavities may lead to identity disorientation, which may last from three to five days, or may be permanent.

It cannot be stressed too often that suicide should also be avoided. Most, though not all, reputable scientific organizations regard suicide as an overwhelming setback in the Search for Self, one that can lead to extreme discouragement and subsequent long-term depression.

And **Do Not** – I repeat, **Do Not** – gaze into a mirror, hoping to peer deep into your soul and discover who you really are. That ain't the way it works, folks.

History and Self

Before proceeding into the body of this work, we must squarely face the matter of your cherished singularity, placing it within a broad historical context.

For this, we surreptitiously captured live on audio two young men who we will call Zek and Zak, dressed in baggy clothes with baseball caps turned backwards, both feeling a little zonked out sitting around at a Mall. The philosophical transcript is herewith reproduced verbatim.

"Hey, Zek? You know, lately, I've been thinking about who I am."

"Whoa, like alert the media."

"It's no joke, man. 'Cause you know it all got like really weird when I thought about who I was. Got deep."

"Ooh major bad."

"Tell me about it. I started thinking about all sorts of crap, like about everyone who has ever lived and walked and talked on the face of the earth. And then I realized."

"… Like, realized …?"

"Realized I'm not the first person to be born and want to know who I am."

"Well, like, duh. Big time."

"No, think about it, man. How many dudes and dudettes over hundreds of centuries have come and gone and been someone before you or me ever came along?"

"You want an exact figure or can I guess?"

"Come on. Just like think about it, think about everyone who has ever existed ... No cheating, think."

"You mean, like think think?"

"Totally. Like close your eyes tight–visualize everyone–and I mean *everyone*, every sucker throughout the ages, before Christ, during Christ, the Middle Ages, *China*."

"Okay. Okay ... Mmmmm ... *Whoa mama!*"

"You see?"

"There are a lot of folks behind my eyes. Like tons and billions and godzillions. I see 'em, man, like lined up, one after another, on top of each other's heads, reaching out into the universe, wrapping around Saturn five times and coming back to earth. We're talking mucho zeros here."

"Now, Zek, like consider the possibility that because so many people have been born and already existed that there really is no one left to be."

(*Note: Here the sound of a distant, wounded animal, a moan slowly rose from Zek's breast, and grew in enormity until it filled the air with a high-whine.*)

"The dawn is breaking over your brow. You understand, Zek, that every identity with every imaginable variation and nuance and individual stamp has lived and walked and talked and been somebody."

(or a reasonable facsimile)

"And when you think about throwing reincarnation into the mix ...."

"Perhaps for the first time in human history we face the likelihood that ... hold it ... everyone's been done. Or at least, everyone worth being ...."

"Oh fuck. Oh fuck. Oh fuck. Then you're saying I could just be imitating someone else who has already like lived and everything?"

"You got it. It's like when you ask yourself, Who am I?, you hear a faint voice from the near or distant past whispering in your ear, 'Who are you? – why, you're me. I was already who you are. Exactly. Down to the very last detail, frowning forehead, nervous tick and all.'"

(Note: a long, long silence.)

"Zippy-fucking-doo-dah man."

"Yeah but you know most people prefer being somebody else so they don't have to worry who they are."

"Yeah, like our parents. And their friends."

"But when I think that I might be like a carbon copy of some ancient being, it's like, soooo discouraging, man."

"Can't get my head around this."

"Oh man."

"Fucking-A."

"You said it."

"Nah, somebody already said that."

"Zippy-fucking-doo-dah man. Fucking-doo-dah."

(Tape runs out at this point.)

The False-Self-Actualization Syndrome
Case Study

The Case

Larry Burt was an overweight forty-three-year-old financial controller for a candy manufacturer who was brought to the Self-Realization, Actualization, Detonation Center in a state of extreme shock and depression.

It appeared that he had looked into the mirror that morning and felt he had come to a complete understanding of who he was; the knowledge had disappointed him.

Once at our Center, he wept copiously and without pause for three straight days. He was given sedatives and laxatives and told bedtime stories in funny voices but nothing seemed to help. At the beginning of the fourth day, I was consulted and was immediately intrigued at the intensity of the crying jag.

"And did you apply the laxatives?" I asked.

"All four varieties."

I was incredulous. "And no results?"

"He's white as a sheet, drinks a lot of liquids and is heard to whimper

Mama mia while looking towards heaven. Other than that, no results."

I asked to see this patient. I marched to Intensive Care, Ward Three, Room Eight, Enter at Own Risk, Third Bed Along, and there he was, Larry Burt.

In appearance, he was unexceptional: balding, plump, a certain bureaucratic roundness to the shoulders. He sobbed, blubbered and moaned, without shame or moderation.

"What is the meaning of this!" I snapped. I have found, in extreme cases of what I term *Self-Knowledge Mania*, that an authoritarian, not to say fascistic intonation, affects wonders. Yet the patient merely raised his head, sniveled, muttered *Mama mia* plaintively, and continued weeping. When I insisted, "What is the meaning of this, sir!" he turned away, retreating in a crouch to a dusty corner[2] in despair.

I pursued him with my questioning, in order to break the spell, bring him around, watch him squirm.

"I have been informed, Mr. Burt, that you have looked into the mirror. Correct?"

He nodded, vaguely. This was the first sign of communication with the outside world he had made in four days.

"And when you looked in the mirror, who exactly did you expect to see?"

He whimpered. He shivered. "My grandfather," he responded hoarsely, "on my mother's side."

"And you didn't see him?"

"No. And I should have known better. He's been dead for

---

[2] It is our longstanding policy to maintain several dusty corners conveniently located throughout the Center's premises, allowing patients who feel a sudden emotional collapse coming on to find quick refuge and solace in these murky sanctuaries.

(or a reasonable facsimile)

years."

"Then who did you see?"

At this, he began to tremble and weep.

"Control yourself and answer my question," I commanded with an impatient stomp of my foot, then added, to increase his trust, "I'm a doctor."

He seemed to shrink further into the dusty corner, sputtering, drooling, emitting unhealthy sounds. His answer came slowly. "*Mm...mm...me* ... oh God!" Larry Burt almost screamed. "*I expected to see me!*"

"And ...?"

And then poured forth a tortured, sob-filled jumble of words from which I could piece together Larry Burt's amazing story of tragic proportions. Here it is, in his own words.

Larry Burt's Own Words

Whenever I have asked myself Who I Am?, I've always fallen asleep. I guess whoever I am is a pretty boring person.

My first memory of this happening was when I was a baby and began to speak. Relatives came over and my mother would sit me in the middle of the room and ask me to say my name in front of everybody. She was proud, I guess, like any mother. She would lean over me, her face like a big moon, and say, "Tell everybody your name, honey. Tell the nice people." I gurgled, I replied, "Larry Burt." And I was right, up to a point. Everyone clapped politely, making approving comments to one another. But when my mother asked me, "And who is that, my little sweetie?" I collapsed, plopped right over on the rug like a limp rag doll. They thought it was epilepsy. They brought in doctors, specialists. They pricked and probed. Some of it hurt, some of it I started to enjoy, but they couldn't find a single thing wrong with me, except when asked who I was, I fell asleep.

From then on, my family avoided asking me any awkward questions concerning my identity or selfhood or what I felt like having for supper. I avoided myself, too. I hurried past mirrors, didn't stay too long alone in the bathroom, yet every time I bent down to tie my shoe, I *knew* whose foot was *really* in that shoe. I don't think anyone can possibly realize what agony I was going through. I was continually running away from myself; yet even after sprinting ten city blocks, *I'd still be there.*

So one day, I came to a compromise with me. In place of self-knowledge, I'd study to become an accountant. I have always worked hard throughout my life, kept to myself, said *Yes* whenever I could to anyone who addressed me, and have been frugal by most people's standards. But dear God, my inner soul has always been so barren. I've always had this sneaky feeling that there was not much of me to know. Maybe one, two modifiers at most.

Then, after many, many years, when I thought I'd forgotten all this, forgot about who I wasn't, really just forgot, I carelessly glanced into the mirror, and that's something I *never, ever do*. Did I half-hope to see my grandfather, on my mother's side, whom I have always admired, and that he would be who I was and offer me some good advice? But he wasn't in the mirror. There was just me, whoever that was. At that instant I had a flash of horrible clarity. It was more intense than sex. Well, almost. I saw who I was. I *knew* who I was.

(Larry Burt halted for some moments to control himself, to wipe away a tear as well as some off-color liquids leaking from his nose.)

"But it took such a short time for me to *know* who I was. I mean, within two seconds, I *knew*, positively, absolutely knew, who I was. Only two seconds worth! I had read all those wonderful things in

(or a reasonable facsimile)

books about the *Self*, where it says it takes some people *years* to know themselves. But me? *A couple of seconds.* I was crushed. The next thing I knew after seeing myself in the mirror, I had blacked out and then woke up here. Honestly, I don't know if anyone can help me now. Really.

Curing Larry Burt
Larry Burt's problem was not so much psychological as fundamental. We at the Center call this the *False-Self-Actualization Syndrome*. Simplified for popular consumption, this syndrome can be explained thusly:

Just as some women can work themselves into a state of Hysterical Pregnancy that exhibits all the outward, biological signs of real pregnancy where none exists, so may a common form of False-Self-Actualization occur in some susceptible minds. While in this state, the individual exhibits all the outward manifestations of one who has just crossed the border into deep self-knowledge, with all its attendant consequences of euphoria followed by mild disappointment.

With this analysis made, Larry Burt was kept under strict supervision at the Center for five months and given a unique set of daily treatments to reveal to him his fundamental error and how it correct it.[3] In the end, running out of tears and drugged to the gills, Larry Burt realized his self-defeating blunder. We successfully erased from his memory any and all thoughts of who he thought he once was. When he finally smiled in his third month of captivity,

---

[3] The techniques utilized in this process are not yet perfected, and, since it remains in its experimental stages, it must be withheld from public and professional scrutiny at this time. However, a paper is in preparation for delivery at next year's International Psychologists Convention in Zurich, Switzerland, with the working title, Retrograde Self-Knowledge, or, Who You Are May Not Be Who You Think You Are, a study of the misapplication of identity in limited sensory organs, such as the brains of Contented Housewives or Corporate Middle Management.

we knew a breakthrough had occurred.

Answering The Question
Before his release, as a final test, Larry Burt was given a mirror to look into. Gulping, hesitating, flocked by medical students with notebooks, he looked into a mirror. His face at first registered shock, then surprise, then a great big smile.

"What do you see, Mr. Burt?"

He looked up at me, tears welling up in his eyes. "My old Granddad," he replied.

He was subjected to a last, pointed question to discover his capacity to deal with the outside world.[4]

"*Who are you?*"

He answered without hesitation, "I am Larry Burt, a man like any other. Willing to admit his mistakes. A man who does not yet truly know himself, but who is still willing to give it another try. I am a man who wishes to contribute to society and his community, and only to look for himself in his spare time with the appropriate medication."

The fact that Larry Burt was able to answer the simple question "Who are you" without falling asleep attested to his current mental health, and he was released into society at large.

Coda
Larry Burt's cure was of an unfortunate short duration. Some weeks later, it appears he suffered a severe relapse, and it was last reported that he was asking people along Highway 101 in California whether or not they had seen Larry Burt lately, and if so, what did he look like?

---

[4] In conformance with State Law.

The Moral Dilemma of Finding Yourself

1. If it feels good, it is good.
    If it feels bad, it is bad.
    If it feels mediocre, you're wasting your time.

2. Pain, in relation to finding yourself, is good. That is why it is a moral dilemma. If you begin to feel bad when you think about who you are, this indicates that you are actually making a decent effort and are on the right track.

    If, on the other hand, it does not hurt, this signifies one of two things:

    > A. Either you are not making a real effort and so are attempting to fool someone (possibly yourself), or,
    > B. You have already found yourself and should not be occupied in creating a moral dilemma where none exists.[5]

---

[5] This, in fact, would be slightly immoral, but that is a different dilemma located in a separate philosophical branch of study. Nevertwwww<n you.

3. Many individuals, upon setting out on the path toward self-enlightenment, often have to give up learned behavior patterns that have survived since childhood. Herman Schmidt gave up his pacifier, even though it was a bright pink. Emily Fipple would not give up her diapers and has consequently abandoned all chances of ever finding herself, at least in this life (although she figures if she's reincarnated as a cockroach or a Mid-Westerner, it'll all be much easier). Jim Dobbs had to give up hoping for his mother and father's love, even though he was an orphan. These are all examples of Moral Dilemmas, although not nearly as interesting as sex.

4. Sex brings us to the question of whether one should make love when one does not know who one truly is. If you make love not knowing who you are, then who is this person making love? You or who? If you reach climax, whose climax is it? If your partner murmurs, "I love you", before, during, or directly after the act of sexual intercourse, when all sorts of hormones are being triggered internally to cause exactly such bonding reactions, to whom exactly are they saying this all-powerful phrase of I love you? To you or to whom they think you are? Here, the Moral Dilemma can only be ignored at your own peril, if your own peril is truly yours, of course. Thus, next time someone says to you bold as brass, "Let's do it, honey", reply thoughtfully, "Who, with me? The real me? Or with the superficial me? The merely physical me? Or the me you think you know or the me you hope I am? The existential me or the spiritual part of me? The me me or simply just me?" You will be surprised at the reactions you will receive by introducing such moral dilemmas into the casual act of recreational sex.

(or a reasonable facsimile)

5. The history of the Moral Dilemma of Finding Yourself goes back at least fifteen centuries, although some people claim it only started on the fifth of last month when someone was in a bad mood.

    The first known example of moral dilemma and self was one Elmer Tug, a ripe Anglo-Saxon sheep dipper who one day didn't know where his boots ended and the sheep-dip began. He solved this by buying new boots. Not all moral dilemmas are so easy to solve. Some are real headaches, such as how do you say aesthetics without sounding effeminate? Other dilemmas remain a complete mystery, such as the purpose of the navel after the womb, or the meaning of death if life is an illusion.

6. The further history of moral dilemmas is interesting if you look at it from the side; an aerial view is also revealing, though there remains a hard-core group who insist on looking at this dilemma from the bottom up. All views are acceptable, yet oddly open to debate. But whichever view you subscribe to, the moral dilemma remains the same: a general pain in the ass.

7. The extended history of the Moral Dilemma as a Pain in the Ass goes back to the beginning of recorded history, and it probably goes back even further but they won't let us look at their notes. But even at the beginning there were tremendous decisions to be made that looked a lot like dilemmas, such as, "What should come first, the 'A' or the 'B'?" And that's just for starters; they hadn't even come to 'G' and 'J' yet, which still confuses many people right into our own times.

    But what has all this got to do with Moral Dilemmas of Finding Yourself? Nothing. Nothing at all. As the great Camus said,

paraphrasing a footnote by Kierkegaard, "Who knows!"
And to which we can only add, "Well, it depends."
On what?
Well, that depends, too.
But that's another essay (and a different dilemma).

How to Find Yourself during Adolescence

You don't.[6]

---

[6] Try it again after you've reached twenty-eight or twenty-nine years of age, or have been married and divorced at least once; it comes to about the same thing. Generally speaking, if you're fifteen, have a lot of pimples, wonder about the existence of God, think your mother and father are just, like, so totally out of it, and your so-called friends seem shallow and conformist, well then, you've got enough to worry about without bringing your innermost being into it. My advice is just do who you seem to be right now, and worry about the rest of who you are when your complexion clears up. Oh, and good luck.

The Role of the Anatomy in the Search for Self

Many people, standing naked before their bathroom mirrors very early in the morning or very, very late at night, often ask themselves in bewildered anguish, "*Who am I?*"[7]

Good question, though perhaps wrong environment.

Nevertheless, in constructing this guide, we were determined to explore every nook and fleshy cranny no matter how iffy the prospects, and thus we approached the staff at the redoubtable Who Am I Clinic based in the suburbs of Dallas, Texas, concerning a controlled anatomical study in selfhood. They shrugged and said, Yeah, sure, why not, could be a giggle.

Environmental Conditions

A group of twenty-one naked people (ten women, ten men, one questionable) were placed in separate, very private cubicles and asked to stand before full-length, one-way mirrors to examine themselves

---

[7] Others may ask, "What am I?", "Is this me?", or "I'm becoming a bit pudgy about the thighs", but these are all mere variations on the basic who-am-I motif.

intimately while the clinic's doctors, totally impartial, observed the goings-on through little cracks in the wall in fascination.

Toes
Many people began with their toes. However, individuals staring at their toes for a long time experienced a skull skin-crawling sensation of omnidirectional dissatisfaction. Many flexed their toes experimentally and when nothing far-reaching seemed to happen in their lives, let alone their souls, they sighed and their eyes drifted from their toes and towards their eyebrows, which they tended to groom in compensation. This behavior may be explained by the fact that toes, by and large, in and among themselves, one next to the other, are not the most inspiring bit of naked anatomy.[8]

Feet
These are frequently referred to as merely the flat things that keep the toes effectively attached to the rest of the anatomy, as well as helping individuals remain upright, mobile, and snigger when tickled.

Ankles
See feet.

Knees
Here the study approached more interesting territory; some of the subjects began to have a bit of tingling, vagueish inner-meaning sensations.[9] However, the knees were not found to be particularly

---

[8] Some of the subjects became inexplicably fixated on the toe just next to the smallest toe, and began wondering, "What *possible* use does that toe have? I don't remember having *ever* used it." The subjects were then reminded via a ghostly voice over an unseen intercom that they had embarked upon a digression in this anatomical search for self and that it was better to speedily proceed to the next bit of anatomy.

[9] Others passed quickly from the knees right to the thighs where they believed more truth lay; yet for a kinky minority, knees were the beginning of their true essence and were not to be knocked.

(or a reasonable facsimile)

aesthetic objects. Yet in their dependable crease and bend, there was a certain philosophical, even fundamental, logic and breath of imagination. Some subjects enjoyed a dawning of self-awareness but were unable to verbalize adequately. Hence, conclusions on the knee as self-stimulators remain ambiguous, while ethics forbid us to pass along any preliminary conclusions, which, if incorrectly applied in the privacy of your own home, could prove slightly degrading, depending on your personal moral code and local city ordinances. As further controlled experiments are carried out, results shall be made public in the pages of the bi-monthly publication, *Psychology Tomorrow, News from the Knees* section.

Thighs

And particularly the back of the thighs. The majority of the subjects found a certain sense of peacefulness while gazing at the rear portion of their thighs in the mirror. Some had startling insights regarding their childhood that they adamantly refused to tell us. One elderly female, however, was heard to exclaim, "So *that's* the meaning of the cosmos."

The Private Parts

Naturally, everyone was extremely eager to pass on to this region and really start finding him or herself. However, due to the nature of this book, which is aimed at the general reader and not to titillate or encourage utterly egocentric behavior, we find that relating the shocking findings of Self and the Crotch Zone would elicit in the broad public a certain—no, we are informed by our lawyer that we are not to go forward and place in cold, hard print exactly what went on. Sorry.[10]

---

[10] Be that as it may, *we're* having a great time reading and re-reading the dirty bits at the laboratory.

Waist and Navel

Hardly anyone could be induced to discover inner meaning in his or her waistline. When urged for some corollary, anything, some subjects turned hostile. One typical remark went, "There's no *real* me in my waist. It's just the place where I hang the top of my pants." Most subjects concurred: the waist possessed too many overtones of daily practicality to warrant any bursts of self-revelation.

The *navel*, as mentioned elsewhere in this book, should not be a place of departure for finding yourself. It is merely a reference point. Several subjects offered pseudomystical, thoroughly unscientific observations on their navels. However, as a courtesy, fifteen minutes were allowed for general navel-gazing, with the only valid comment worthy of note being, "It's sort of like watching TV." Yet, for the record, we include some of the subjects' valuations concerning the immediate, though *not* lasting effects of naval-gazing:

"I feel a real sense of inner knowledge."
"I feel a real sense of outer knowledge."
"How did all that lint get in there!"
"I want to go back to my private parts."
"The mystery of existence."
"Why me?"
"Why you?'
"Uh-oh …."

Chests and Breasts

Women tended to examine their breasts and feel a warm sense of evolutionary purpose and meaning.

Men tended to look at their nipples and experience a much suppressed breast-envy neurosis, which quickly evolved into philosophical ramblings, wondering why natural selection had slipped up and left them with nonfunctional nipples.

(or a reasonable facsimile)

The Neck
See Feet, same principle.

The Head
Every subject had a particular fascination with the head. Many were observed to turn it from left to right, and vice versa, plumbing the depths. People were observed to pull their chins, flick their earlobes and stick out their tongues as they searched for themselves. Only two and a half subjects succeeded in discovering themselves in this manner and were given permission to go home.

One subject found only half of himself; he worked the nightshift on an automotive assembly line; he said he would return to the clinic next week and pick up the rest of him if he could get time off.

One subject stared into his left nostril for some minutes before declaring, "I ... I think I see someone."

Another person turned her head away from the mirror, then look back really quickly, in this way experimentally trying to find herself while she wasn't looking.[11]

Yet another subject glared at herself in the mirror and demanded fiercely, "I know you're in there somewhere ... come out, you coward ... come on, I dare you...."

One subject was caught trying to twist his head off his neck, mumbling, "I know, I *know* if I could just get this off I'd finally set myself free and know who I am.[12]

A last subject stared glumly at himself, muttering, "I don't believe it. This is modern science? Pristine experimental setting. Supposedly the latest in technology and government grants. Yet here I am, a well-paid, middle-aged banking executive naked in front of a mirror being observed for insight and significance. And I

---

[11] We sent her home, too.

[12] He was remanded into custody and held over for a few days extra observation.

pay taxes for this....?"

Upon concluding these experiments, the subjects were excused to go home, or back to their places of businesses, or the mental institutes who'd loaned them out to us for a while at little or no expense, while the researchers, doctors and medical students and a few social engineers and one plain housewife added for a touch of color, retired to their labs for the following eighteen months in order to study and marshal analytical data relating to the results following different lines of investigation. In the end, they admitted only to a few hesitant conclusions that could only be verified by further experiments.

Government grants have been secured.

Business and Identity
Case Study

There have been volumes written, published, and consumed on the techniques and fundamentals of business: business as a way of life, a way of being, a replacement for being. There are thousands, even millions, who seek identity through business. Identity, however, should really be approached as more than just a nine-to-five proposition. Ideally, it should be a round-the-clock occurrence.

Believe it or not, there are people who get up in the morning not knowing who they are. They wash and eat breakfast actively shunning who they are—they travel to work with blank looks on their faces—and only when reaching their place of employment and going directly to their usual spot of occupancy, will a strange anxiety be quieted. They become Joe Blow or Suzy Nothing, desk five, cubicle thirty. They disappear into paperwork. They gossip. They worry about promotions. They are competitive and eat lots of sugared foods. Some are known to eagerly accept overtime, work through lunch and even to come in on Saturdays. These are hard-core Business Identity Substitutes and are usually pleasant, energetic, have prematurely grey hair and die at an early age. They also happen to make a lot of money, which some people think is much more fun than finding yourself.

As an illustration of this point, I offer the following excerpts from the diary of one Mr. Betts, a former junior executive at one of our more formidable multinational corporations.

After a promising quick rise in the business world, Mr. Betts was stricken with Doubt, a usually fatal frame of mind within the business community. On the sly, Mr. Betts sought therapy and, due to a particularly fragile nature, his defense system rapidly fell into disarray and he was institutionalized. After intense psychotherapy, he developed a radical reaction to his own previous lifestyle.

Below, we present selected portions of his diary documenting his state of mind during this time.

June 2nd

The haze is clearing. I'm beginning to understand.

Most of my life I've possessed a driving urge to be a suit and tie. Even as a boy, I would sneak into my parent's bedroom, put a tie round my neck, finger my father's pinstriped suit, and fall into a reverie. I would pretend to compose memos, make decisions, and abuse my subordinates. Once, in childish curiosity, I did experiment with putting on my mother's jewelry and underwear, and, although a somewhat pleasing, tranquil-making pastime, wanting to be a size 36-D brassiere just didn't come close to the *zing* and *boom* of being a suit and tie.

It never occurred to me to sit down and ask myself, Who Am I? Instead, I wondered what it would take to get into the Harvard Business School. The essence of my being was the bottom line.

Nowadays, I have a totally different perspective. I find it very strange that people willingly say, 'Hi, I'm Jones from IBM. I'm

(or a reasonable facsimile)

Schmidt from XYZ. I'm Harvey of ABC.' Most of my acquaintances have turned permanently into suits and ties: it's become more important to them which acronym they represent rather than who they are.

And that's where I've been. That's where I've come from.

But now I'm Betts from nowhere–unemployed but in sure possession of self-knowledge.

The question remains, what type of job can I get with this qualification?

June 3rd

Went for my first interview today. Was questioned about my qualifications.

"You've put down on your application, Mr. Betts, that you know yourself," observed the gently smiling Human Resources Executive.

"Yes, that's true. I know who I am."

"I can understand your pride in the matter. Only, shouldn't this particular information be with your Personal History and not under Previous Experience and Qualifications?"

"Well, it's what I feel I do best."

"Know yourself?"

"Yes."

"And that's what you're looking for? A job in knowing yourself? And what do you think your salary requirements would be? Really, Mr. Betts...."

I was not offered a position.

But now that I've given up Anglo-Saxon Capitalistic Materialism, I find the one thing I do really well, and enjoy doing endlessly, is knowing myself. I wish I could find a job where self-knowledge is a career. This lack clearly demonstrates the shortsightedness of modern society's structure.

June 12th
What is the *use* of self-knowledge? The practical use?

I've been the rounds of over a dozen potential employers and not one of them has been seriously interested in my self-knowledge. Indeed, some are outright mocking about it!

"So you've found yourself, Mr. Betts. What did you do, lose it? Did you fasten a collar around its neck, reading, 'In case of loss, please return to owner'?"

"My God, Mr. Betts, you know yourself! I'm sorry, but although we are an equal opportunity employer, we only hire confused people."

"Hmm ... self-knowledge ... do you have a diploma for this? What might be the final examination for this sort of thing: 'To the best of your ability, do you remember when you first noticed your navel and what impact it had on your later life?' Really, Mr. Betts, I'm sure you're a nice person, but do you really know your ass from a hole in the ground?"

June 28th
More interviews. More abuse.

"Here, Mr. Betts, you're required to cook food fast—we have no available facilities and very little time for our employees to sink suddenly into an introspective reverie while the buns are burning."

I'm not certain how long my self-respect and sensitive nature can take this. The crass commercial world is gnawing away.

June (July)
More of the same, only more so. Strange. It's all so strange. I feel strange.

(or a reasonable facsimile)

July 31st
I don't believe it.

July 32nd
I still don't believe it.

August 5th through 20th
I think I'm starting to believe something.

The week before last
My brains are beginning to melt. I put in earplugs.

Day after Yesterday
Doctor came to visit me today, but I wouldn't come out of the closet. After all, I have all my friends in here. The pussycat that doesn't move any more, a torn T-shirt from my childhood, two funny bent matches, and a couple of minutes left of an all-day sucker.

How could I leave all my little friends? I'd been telling them all about myself for days, and they listened and seemed to understand …

Then the doctor sent in two very large people and after a long time they found me in my secret place in the corner and they grabbed me by my self-knowledge but I wouldn't let go.

Soon, though, I forgot everything and turned into a vegetable deep in the ground waiting for Spring.

It must be admitted that some naysayers in the business world claim that while a little self-knowledge is a dangerous thing, a lot of self-knowledge can be terminal. This, I am happy to point out, is still open to debate.

A Debate among Business Executives in a Major Corporation
"Self-knowledge is an indulgent luxury. Tell me if I'm wrong, but I see it as a dog-eat-dog world out there, and it's better if you study closely the size of the other guy's canines rather than your Self."

"I usually just take two aspirins."

"It's the result of a permissive education. They put too much emphasis on individual integrity and not enough on collective integration."

"Last time I took two aspirins, they gave me a headache, so I took two more aspirins and that gave me a stomach ache, then I took two more aspirins because the room was wobbling, then I took some more aspirins and woke up in the hospital, a tube up my nose and a hose down my throat. Isn't that an interesting insight?"

"Shut-up, Hopkins."

"Yes, sir."

"Why can't there more employees like Hopkins? He's servile, meticulous, and we've got him by the nuts; except for the occasional overdose, he's an ideal worker. Where are the major corporations going to find a high caliber of people if everyone gets a notion in their heads to start asking metaphysical questions about themselves which no one can give a practical answer to?"

"Perhaps Free Radicals are beaming down Self-Doubt from their satellites?"

"My suspicions exactly."

"Yes."

"Hmm ...."

"Harrumph!"

"Anyone have an aspirin?"

The Subconscious versus the Unconscious in the Search for Self
Maggie Debrie, Syndicated Columnist

Well, Then

I am glad to be given this opportunity to discuss this fascinating subject in some depth. In my daily column "Dear Maggie, Please!" I must keep answers to most problems straight, practical, helpful, oversimplified, and, if possible, something you can whistle a happy tune to. But letters keep coming across my desk every week concerning this Subconscious versus Unconscious business. Demanding advice in the nicest possible way, for the most part (only I just wish Melanie DeSmet from Belgium would *cut it out*!).

I always say it is best to begin with questions. We all know there's a self. Somewhere inside. But where, exactly? Is there a precise location? Or is it just floating around in the breeze like some colorful aura that only certain people can see, people with a special gift or mental imbalance (hug that person!).

Many people crave simple directions about where they should

How to Find Yourself

be looking for the Self, in the Subconscious or the Unconscious. This is a Big Question, and I think I have some Good Answers.

Examples are always best. Here is a letter I actually received that confidently began:

> After what seems years of searching, I found myself today, and it was in my Unconscious all the time! I'd never thought to look in there. It was like the last time I misplaced my iron and couldn't find it—I don't know *how* it got into the shoe closet, it was the last place I thought to look! Anyway, since unexpectedly finding myself in my Unconscious, I've cut down on my smoking tremendously and have gained weight and yet still feel comfortable with myself although I don't like the way this pudgy stuff gathers round my tummy....

Yet all too often I receive letters like the following:

> Dear Maggie:
> I'm lost!
> I've been looking for myself all day and I'm nowhere to be found!
> And dinner isn't even begun and the family's going to storm in at any minute.
> And if they ask me what I've been doing all day, what can I answer?
> The truth? Looking for myself? They'd only laugh. All sixteen of them.
> I'm desperate, Maggie. I need help. It's humiliating to look for yourself and never be there.
> And you always feel alone. Especially when you're alone.
> Perhaps if I found myself I wouldn't be so lonely. At least I'd have someone to talk to.

(or a reasonable facsimile)

> Maggie, I feel like you're my friend, I read you religiously, and since I've turned everywhere I can think of and I'm nowhere to be found, could you clear something up for me? Yesterday, I overheard some people at the shopping mall mention the Subconscious. I gathered that someone had recently found herself there.
> Could this possibly be true? Is there any chance that I too might be in my Subconscious? If so, how do I get in? And what will I look like? Should I have a formal dress on when I go into the Subconscious or are sweatpants good enough? What's the etiquette? You must know. You know so much.
> Please answer quickly. It's urgent. All my friends seem to be finding themselves lately and I feel so left out.
> Mary B. of Halcyon, Montana

Then I received this revealing letter from Susan H. of Waterlog, Oregon:

> Maggie, I spent ten solid years looking for myself in my Subconscious. Unsuccessfully. Then one day, idle and in a rut, I looked into the Unconscious and what do you know, but there I was, all smiles, waiting patiently!
> I share this information so your many readers might benefit from my experience (and I found you can wear sweatpants when finding yourself. It's usually a very casual affair).

Well, in our hectic modern lives, people place an increasing value on finding themselves. A spate of self-help books addressing the matter are bombarding the public, while universities have been pumping out therapists at the rate of hundreds a week just to cope with the demand.

How to Find Yourself

In short, there's been a heck of a lot of hullabaloo on the subject, and now that the marketing people have gotten their hands on the who-are-you industry, it's harder than ever to separate the wheat from the chaff. The you from the who.

Okay, Then
So first things first™, as I always say: let's clear up the primary question of *how* the Subconscious is different from the Unconscious.

As always in such matters, I reached for my trusty dictionary, and it read, in part:

> Subconscious: an entity or part of the mental apparatus overlapping, equivalent to, or distinct from the Unconscious! (Exclamation mark mine.)
> Unconscious: the absolute principle of the universe according to the doctrine of panpneumatism? (Question mark mine.)

I put the dictionary aside with a sense of disappointment.

Ingesting a mass of material of reputable experts, I concluded that the Subconscious is best entered during waking hours, whereas the Unconscious is more accessible when on the edge of sleep, although there are no ironclad rules.

I tend to lean toward the Unconscious as the key in the matter because it is probably harder to get at and thus more suffering is involved.[13] You see, if we agree that the Self resides within the Unconscious, Seekers risk a good deal of frustration, if, just on the edge of sleep, they ask themselves ask who they are and, right as the answer is forthcoming, fall asleep. Well, imagine if this happens

---

[13] Suffering is always character building, if done in moderation and writing me a detailed letter about it afterwards.

(or a reasonable facsimile)

night after night! We could have a nation of insomniacs, afraid to go to sleep in fear that they might miss finding themselves!

As I've stated so often in my regular, syndicated newspaper column: *Life is not easy!*™.

But always remember *never be defeated* (™ pending).

Well, Well

Being a practical gal, I want to examine *Ways of Entering the Unconscious*.

One of the best suggestions as to how to gain entrance to the Unconscious was put forth by Mrs. Beryl G., of Fargo, North Dakota. I quote her letter at length, because of what I believe is its instructive value.

> Maggie, don't think I'm foolish, but here's what's worked for me. I just asked myself and asked myself, day in and day out, Who am I? Who am I? Who am I? My plan was to try and wear down my resistance. At first, just as I suspected, I refused to respond. But I knew if I kept at it, something would come of it, sometime, someday, some sort of me.
> Well, finally, one day, I got bored asking myself, Who am I? over and over like an idiot, and gave myself an answer, just any old thing, to shut me up. I kept doing that for a year or two.
> And then I realized all at once that when I uttered an actual answer, I should maybe study my answers, and carefully. I asked myself, Who I was again, gave an answer, and looked to see whether the answer sounded right, sounded like something I could be. If it didn't—and in the beginning hardly any answer I gave sounded

anything like me—I'd reject it and go back to asking me, Who am I? Who am I?

I can't begin to tell you how many crazy answers I told myself over the next months. I was General George Washington chopping down his cherry tree—that wasn't me. A snake charmer in a Calcutta slum—no way. A reincarnation of a Buddhist Monk working in a leper colony—ugg! I wondered if I wasn't a successful physiologist with a chain of fitness centers around the world—I liked that idea, but I'm an overweight semidisabled divorcee with three teenage children, so that wasn't the real me.

Anyway, I could feel myself, day by day, getting closer and closer. I was progressing. And then, one day, boom, just like that! I happened.

I'd asked myself for the umpteenth time, Who am I?, and I'd replied as usual, the first silly thing that popped into my brain, but this time, upon examining the answer, it sounded half-reasonable. My heart swelled. But being no dummy by now, I investigated the answer very carefully. But no matter what angle I examined it from I could find no holes, no leaks, no false scent. I began to hope I'd found myself.

For the next few days, I practiced the answer on my intimate friends and close family members. After receiving many positive responses (only a couple of people laughed), I experimented in public at the supermarket, the hairdressers, telling people who I was. From nearly every corner came back praise and congratulations. Lots of positive feedback. I felt fulfilled, and satisfied. I felt like who I was meant to be.

(or a reasonable facsimile)

And for five years I was happy. Very.
Then recently my world unexpectedly went topsy-turvy. Again, just like that (funny how life can be like that). One day I woke up and discovered I'd forgotten myself. The answer to Who I Was was suddenly gone! Whoosh! Clear out of my mind! Like it had never existed. I hadn't bothered to write me down because I never thought for one moment that such things happened. Once I discovered me, I'd assumed I just always be me. Not true. I tried and tried to remember Who I Was, but somehow, that fateful night, my Unconscious took away my identity and locked it up somewhere deep and hidden again.
I was understandably depressed and alienated from my Unconscious for the following days. I let the laundry go. Ate too many fried foods. Yelled at the kids, locked them in the closet, just blubbered. But I never let anything get me down very long. I decided I just had to get back to work and start asking myself, Who am I? and begin all over again the laborious process of elimination. I let the kids out to go play.
I've been back at it a while now—Who am I? Who am I?—but haven't had much luck yet. But I'm hopeful. I do want to advise those who might take up my mode of self-discovery to always, always carry a portable tape recorder to document your every answer. Then, if ever you find yourself, you'll have it on tape, and if, like me, you should wake up one day not you again, you can turn on the tape recorder and There You Are!
It'll be a hell of a time saver, believe you me.
I would like to thank Beryl for sharing that with us.

How to Find Yourself

Oh Well

What is the Unconscious? The dictionary (that increasingly suspect tome) defines the Unconscious as a noun, which any schoolgirl can tell you is either a person, place or thing. Well, let's take a closer look at this!

The Unconscious is not a person. As far as I know, no one has ever been introduced to someone who is the Unconscious, and those who *do* sometimes introduce themselves as the Unconscious have been quickly unmasked as mere pranksters or juvenile delinquents.

Nor is the Unconscious a place. I know; I've consulted many maps. Some people claim the Unconscious is located in the farmlands of Northern Uppsalla, but I've encountered several individuals from that region and they appeared perfectly normal to me.

Finally, the Unconscious is not a thing, although this is slightly more difficult to refute in a snappy sentence or two. Everything in Existence, both Earthly and Universal, has not necessarily been discovered and classified, so many things do exist that we just don't know about, so the Unconscious may very well be a thing out there, or in there, hiding. But modern humankind has searched the furthest ends of the Amazon, and even been to the moon and back several times to get more rocks just to make sure that's all there is up there, so I really do think that if the Unconscious was a thing, we'd have located it by now.

I don't know where the dictionary gets off so brazenly declaring that the Unconscious is a noun. There isn't a shred of evidence.

Well

I hope all this has helped. The Unconscious, for all its infuriating vagueness, is probably where each of you are. I mean, the Subconscious, like the prefix Sub- indicates, is a place "down

(or a reasonable facsimile)

there," and like most places *down there*, it is either dirty or has sexual connotations, by which I mean dirty, dark, moist. And feels funny when you wash it. Even if you do it really quickly. Especially if you do it really quickly. So stay out of there! Just be the best Unconscious Being you can be.

And that's my advice.

See you in my column, *Dear Maggie–Please!*™.

Onanistic Bliss as a Pathway to the Soul
Live, from Radio KAKA, California

"Good morning, ladies and gentlemen, and I hope there are no children in the listening audience. This is D.D. Remington coming at you live from radio KAKA with Joe 'Hands and Fingers' Quik, renowned self-abuser of notorious proportions. As we like to say here at Radio KAKA, we will go to any lengths to entertain our listeners with the most bizarre garbage on our regular 10 a.m. program, 'How I Found Myself and Proud of It'. Here in the studio to have a little chat with what makes Joe 'Hands and Fingers' Quik, go—and come. Mr. Quik, good morning."

"Hi ya."

"How are you this morning?"

"Well, you caught me right between some pretty heavy-duty onanism sessions, so I'm a little out of breath, but okay enough. How's yourself?

"Involved in a healthy, mature, monogamous, heterosexual relationship with the mother of my children within the socially acceptable confines of a nuclear family."

"Oh. Is this going to be one of those interviews? All judgmental and condemning before investigating the positive aspects of my alternative lifestyle."

"Hey, Mister Slippery Fingers, no need to be defensive if you're really proud of your chronic behavior. That is, of course, unless you are carrying a great burden of guilt."

"I don't carry any burdens of guilt. I discharge them regularly."

"I bet you do. For the record, may I see your hands?"

"Sure. No problem."

"Hmm. Thank you. I was just checking an old wives tale ... you don't shave your hands regularly, do you?"

"No, but I do have a group of warts I can't get rid of."

"We'll pass over that. Since this program is known for focusing on various systems individuals in our troubled society utilize in the search to find themselves, I must say, with all due hostility, it's difficult to see how this messin' with your private parts in a regular, systematic, obviously highly neurotic way, has helped you to find yourself."

"It's my outlet to get me inside. We all know how you have to struggle with yourself to find out who you are. I've simply selected a specific part of my anatomy to struggle with, to come to grips with, so to speak."

"Day after day?"

"Day in, day out. But my onanistic bliss technique energizes me. It's true I sometimes do head down what at first seems a fruitful avenue of self-exploration, only to discover a dead end. It's an endless search, pulling and pushing yourself to the edge of who you are. Like anything else, there's lots of false starts and encouraging glimpses of pure enlightenment."

"Yeah. Right. Sounds like you've been into this—into yourself— for some time now. Exactly how long have you been abusing your

(or a reasonable facsimile)

private parts?"

"Oh, for about as long as I can remember. It's hereditary. My ancestors have been traced."

"Oh. So this way of exploring who you are has been ... handed down to you ... in a manner of speaking."

"You've got that tone of voice again."

"You mentioned your ancestors. Tell us about them."

"Well, my father's the best place to start. These rites of onanistic bliss all started when my father entered an Artificial Insemination Center for Advanced Fertilization ..."

He entered the building, combing his hair, looking around expectantly, and went directly to the counter. A serious woman stood there.

"Yes?" she inquired.

"Hi."

"May I help you?"

"I sure hope so. Is this First National Feminist Sperm Bank of Southern California? As it says in this newspaper article?" He held out a clipping he had cut out of the Sunday Edition of that paper.

"Yes, it is."

"Well, hey, I'm here to open an account. And I'd like to deposit immediately. Is there a feminist available?"

"Excuse me?"

"This is the Feminist Sperm Bank, isn't it? I've got the sperm, you've got the Feminists, I want to deposit."

"I think—"

"In fact, I think I'm pretty well equipped to make multiple deposits."

"I see."

"In fact, I think I'm able to make multiple deposits in multiple accounts each day for the next six months. And that's just short term. If the interest rate's good here, we could probably start thinking long term, and whenever you open any other branches, I can go and deposit like hell, get things rolling in new territory. And if you open up branches internationally, I'll go deposit there, too. Hope you expand into France. Boy, I'd really like to deposit with some French Feminists."

"Listen—"

"I know, I know. First I have to prove my solvency—hey, I'm a serious, dedicated entrepreneur who thinks that a sperm bank is just the damned best idea you Feminists ever came up with. Hey, you're kinda cute. Are you a sperm teller? You take deposits?"

"I think you're under a grave misapprehension."

"Nah! I've never been sick a day in my life."

"This is strictly a cooperative feminist health care and financial center. We help infertile couples, lesbians or single women who want children."

"Hey, if you're open-minded, I'm open-minded."

"All right, if you insist." She took out some forms. "After passing a physical examination, your height, weight, race, blood type and other genetic characteristics will be noted. We will then accept your sperm—"

"This is the part I've been waiting for," he said, smacking his palms together.

"If your seed is found suitable, you will be paid a fee for each deposit, and that will be the end of all legal obligations. We will use your spermatozoon to artificially inseminate—"

"Hold on. Artificially what?"

"In-sem-i-nate. Please listen carefully. We here at First

(or a reasonable facsimile)

National Feminist Sperm Bank of Southern California don't like to repeat ourselves."

"We're getting off the track. I'm a willing customer, and I just want to deposit. We won't talk high finance at this point. No stocks, no bonds. Let's just talk savings book deposits, except in this case the savings book is a savings woman, har-har!"

The Feminist at the counter became more severe, less charmed. "I'm sorry, all dealings here are strictly private, between the donor and his conscience. There is no physical contact between males who donate their seed and female customers who eventually purchase said seed."

"Wait a sec. We're off the track again. What's this seed business?"

"If you wish to leave a seed specimen with us for evaluation, you may do this by taking this glass container into that soundproof cubicle over there and ejaculate therein. Cork immediately and return specimen. Pictorial pornography is available upon request. As stated, you will be asked to fill out certain forms, and we'll be in touch with you."

"Hold it another sec. This is getting a mite weird. You saying you want me to take this here test tube into the next room there and show it a good time?"

"That is regular procedure."

"No hugging and kissing then?"

"Not relevant. All that is required is mere mechanical expulsion. We are only concerned with the sperm count in your fluid. All semen expulsions are attained purely by your own manual and mechanical manipulation."

"Hey, I never mechanically expulsed anything! I'm a terrific lover. I can give references."

"That may be, but carnal techniques are of no interest

51

here."

"Hey, come on. Between you and me, no woman has ever come up to me and said, 'Hey baby, let's go to bed, you look like great sperm count'."

"As stated, that is our regular procedure."

"Maybe here, but where I come from, we're into flesh and blood—animal instincts, you know? Grr. Roar. Unless ... unless you got someone in that cubicle over there. A feminist who, uh, helps fiddle around and bring a man a certain satisfaction. Now that I could handle. Someone handling me, har-har."

"I'm sorry, no."

"You mean ... you want me to fiddle my diddle until I go whoopee?"

"Whatever terminology you prefer and is readily grasped by your educational level."

"Oh man, woman ... I don't know. I'm sorely tempted to take my deposits elsewhere." Then he made his decision, taking the flask. "Well ... I came all the way. And I'm sure, once you see the quantity, check out the quality, they'll be plenty of real women-folk who'll want the real thing. So, okay then, just this once though."

"... And that's how it all started. Doing it once was all it took for my dad. Habit wasn't far behind. Addiction thereafter. Then a steady evolution from mere self-abuse to something more engendering and socially acceptable—total and absolute self-gratification. And by the time I came along, the habit had become genetic. And now we're setting up the "Self-knowledge through Self-Gratification" franchises, going global, just as my father once dreamed. Just goes to show you, the American Way is not dead. Work at something

(or a reasonable facsimile)

hard and long enough, never give up, no matter how tough the battle or exhausting the effort, you can follow your dream and make it come true. The American Dream spurts on!"

"Well, that's all we have time for here at Radio KAKA, California, this morning. Thank you for your story."

"You're welcome." He extended his hand.

"Do you mind if we skip the shaking hands bit?"

"Okay. Uh. Would you mind directing me to your radio station's bathroom? I'm feeling a bit–"

"Don't tell me. Just head straight down that hallway–"

And he raced out, hot and bothered.

"Well, Mister and Ms Radio Listening Audience, you heard it here first, and probably for the last time. And remember to tune in same time, same station tomorrow, with me, D.D. Remington, live from the studio, for more weird and occasionally wondrous tales in our "How I Found Myself and Proud of It" program. And now for the weather in your region—"

How to Do Introspection
Sir Roger Thornsworth III

Introspection Abused

Of all the tools utilized in the search for Self, that of Introspection is perhaps the most widely misused.

People tend to use introspection for essentially trivial matters, such as which type of shirt or blouse to wear, which sort of perfumed toilet paper to buy, or which words to murmur to one's lover? The abuse possibilities are boundless.

All self-seekers should understand that introspection is a delicate, Olympian instrument requiring constant nurturing. Would you use a thousand-dollar note to wipe your nose? Normally not. So then why use precious introspection in the same manner, such as when thinking about the evening meal? How often have you spent time considering, "Hamburgers are all very well and fine, but what about pork chops? And the merits of roast chicken are not to be sniffed at?" *This is a shallow waste of introspection.* Hell, stick with the hamburgers!

The introspection tool can go flaccid with such banal overuse.

After a day of introspection wasted on what tie to wear or which pair of shoes goes with which belt, *how* can you believe that after returning home and eating your hamburgers or pork chops you can begin a serious session of introspection? The tool has become completely sapped of its energy and life force.

If you insist on using introspection in this manner, and one day when you really need to know who you are, the only answer you'll find will be mashed potatoes.

The solution to this is easy-peasy. The majority of your daily decisions should be made using your *impulses*. That's why Nature evolved them. Impulses are for essentially superficial activities, such as eating, lovemaking, creating art, vacuuming the rug or office work, whereas introspection is for your soul. Your very soul.[14]

Approaching Introspection

You must not be brusque with Introspection. By nature it is a somewhat anxious, distressed entity. Introspection needs to be treated gingerly, with good preparation for its use made well in advance, at least one hour minimum, but three hours are preferable.

Such preparations are performed by repeating to yourself, "I am going to wonder who-I-am and what-it's-all-about in three hours time." This way the tool becomes well lubricated before use. It is highly recommended that you remind yourself of the forthcoming coming introspection session, say, every ten to fifteen minutes.[15]

There remains a hard-core school of so-called mental health experts who promote the notion that the act of introspection is

---

[14] Really, I can't make it any plainer than that.

[15] Naturally, all preparatory phrases should be repeated silently, as befits introspection. It has been proven that if others nearby hear you repeat such phrases as "Introspection will commence in 45 minutes, 25 seconds," your social life will tend to take a wicked plunge, and your mental health becomes suspect. This is due to general *Introspection Ignorance*.

(or a reasonable facsimile)

best done on the spur of the moment, as when one suddenly for no reason at all "falls into thought". This is basically an amateurish attitude and will get you nowhere, at least nowhere you really want to go.

Depth in introspection is a holistic concept, which should not be confused with the Holly Concept, which is usually only done on Christmas Eve, among relatives, before an open fire, and is not usually illegal. True Depth, however, as a holistic concept, is perfectly legal if done between consenting adults, although it has been known on occasion to corrupt minors. But that's the chances you take.

To sum up: Introspection is a skittish instrument, to be approached with understanding, a kind look, and inquiring politely as to its health. You should never launch yourself at it brutishly: "Okay, gimme an insight!" Introspection will tend to just shrivel up if such brutal methods are employed.

Historical Roots
The history of Introspection tends to have intense periods where a great deal of introspection took place, such as during the Renaissance or whenever interest in organized religion began to flag. On the other hand, there have been times when hardly anyone thought, such as the Middle Ages or the beginning of this book.

Formal Introspection was first proposed by one Pious the Backward in the court of Eleanor the Snooze near Gibraltar around the time the swallows came back once and for all. Pious the Backward stated, "God hath given us a tool by which we may ask, *Why?* Unfortunately, he did not include a mental tool which adequately answers this *Why?* Usually we simply respond, *Why not?* which is self-evidently insufficient, not to mention just a tad disappointing.

Why needs further in-depth consideration." This convinced Queen Eleanor the Snooze of the worthiness of his ideas, and awarded Pious the Backward a ten-year grant in *Why Research*, research that has evolved to its present state of activity, where many tenured academics in *Why* receive many different grants.[16]

Introspection Generally
Introspection is a specific tool used for the specific purpose of General Knowledge of One's Innermost Being, or Who You Are—whichever comes first. It's width and breadth are astounding, especially if you're sitting down and looking up.

Techniques for Introspection
Introspection, it bears repeating, should be approached from the outside in. Rare is the case where one starts from one's innermost being and works toward a shallower understanding of oneself.

So, let's actually do some introspection. Let us assume you are sitting and things are quiet. You have had time to yourself and are not expecting any urgent interruptions. I shall also assume that your approach has been orthodox—you've been quiet, friendly, yet firm with your introspection, and your three-hour introductory comments have relaxed you for forthcoming search for self.

You begin your first descent into innermost being by applying a Zen technique known as *know-nothing*. You do this by emptying your mind of everything and seeing what's left. If there is truly nothing there, you may assume you've successfully arrived at the First Level of Introspection.

To arrive at the Second Level of Introspection, you must

---

[16] Interestingly, no one has ever satisfactorily answered *Why* for good and all. It has merely been bureaucratized into a lucrative careerism by creating numerous offshoots and in general avoiding the answer by creating new problems. And why not?

(or a reasonable facsimile)

now introduce a thought, otherwise you risk one of two things occurring: you will either become bored or fall asleep. So, introduce a thought. Carrots, for instance. (Granted, carrots are not, in and of themselves, a very appealing topic, but they do have their uses, such as being considered excellent brain food, and they have that nice nonthreatening bunny color about them. In any case, do utilize a somewhat sedate and unintoxicating subject, for the brain's deeper, energetic faculties must be kept for the Third Level.)

Once past carrots (or any other fruit or vegetable), one enters the Third Level, and this is where things really start popping. Here, certain individuals may commence to hallucinate weirdly and this alarming state should be combated by taking two aspirins immediately and returning to the carrot state until the condition stabilizes.

Other individuals may see flashes of light which are commonly referred to as *flashes of light*. This is a good sign. Keep watching. Many times, flashes of light turn into flashes of insight, and hence a great deal of valuable groundwork is being done here.

Once you have collected at least five flashes of insight *minimum* (or twenty-five flashes of light, convertible), you may now descend to the Fourth, and final level, of Introspection, commonly referred to as Timelessness, or a metaphysical type of catnap.

Rare is the case where you will encounter yourself in all your naked glory the first time at this level; but if you do, don't panic or be shocked: many people look this way in the Timelessness state. In any event, you may be surprised at the unexpected things that come to mind (I know I was).

The length of time spent at this depth is variable, depending on the individual's experience and ambitions. Be advised not to find too much of yourself at one time; leave some over for subsequent journeys to your soul.

How to Find Yourself

Once you're satisfied about who you are—or just plain sick and tired—wave goodbye and get out of yourself. Unlike the slow, delicate descent into Introspection, resurfacing is much easier. All you have to do is open your eyes. If the result is not completely satisfactory and you still have vague flashes of insight or crave carrots, go to the kitchen and wash a utensil, or fed a pet, play a tune on the harmonica, something manual and down to earth. The effect is usually swift and effective.

Upon returning to normalcy, you may assess your work for the day, and who you are, and be proud. This concludes your voyage of Introspection, and is appropriately called *A Fulfilling Experience Requiring Endless Repetition*.

How to Find Yourself through (or in spite of) Marriage
Case Study

The Love Story of Doreen Yip and Alexander Ha
When this couple became engaged, Doreen Yip, a modern woman of independent temperament, insisted she be recognized as a unique individual in her own right.

"Honey-munchkins, I don't want to live through your achievements and take on your identity," she declared to her fiancé, Alexander Ha, who wore the mournful face typical of the modern male when face with a modern woman.

In touch with his feminine side whether he liked it or not, he weighed her words, attempting enlightenment. "Of course you don't want to be called Mrs. Ha. That's fine with me, honey-bunch-kins. You just stay Ms. Yip."

"No," she answered after a moment's thought, dissatisfied with this compromise, "you don't understand, you old silly-willy. I do want to be identified *with* you, that is what a partnership is about, yet I don't wish to become identified *because* of you."

Being supportive, Alexander Ha tried again. "So, at social occasions you'd prefer not to be introduced as Mr. Ha and Ms. Yip?"

"No, not really–"

"Miss Yip and Mr. Ha?" he suggested hopefully.

"Not that either."

"Ms. Yip-Ha?"

"Definitely not."

As sometimes happens, even with a consciousness raised beyond the norm, irony creeps into a male's tone.

"Then how about if you're introduced as Mrs. Ha and I'm introduced as Mr. Ha, then we can be known as Mr. and Mrs. Ha-Ha."

"That's not funny," she said. "And I don't want to become a laughingstock."

Commentary

This is only the merest tip in the complex and ever-changing condition of man and woman and modern identity.

In the good old days, way back when, Man had dominated Woman for centuries and all was blissful, if a little tense, she sublimated her cravings into the Pots and Pans Syndrome, while he went gallivanting off on Crusades in foreign lands to loot and burn many villages and have all the fun.

Then modern times arrived and the real trouble began.

Science must take a substantial part of the blame. The Ancients believed man's sperm was the be-all and the end-all of creation, and that the male instrument shooting sperm into the world was as mighty as the day is long, if not longer. *Woman*, however, was basically a convenient, fleshy nine-month incubator. Then modern science had to go and discover ovaries. And their eggs. Sperm, it

(or a reasonable facsimile)

turned out, was a relatively minor though essential ingredient in baby making. And there seemed to be a lot of it to go around. Young males could churn this stuff out every couple of hours, no problem. So compared to ovaries, cyclic eggs and those amazing nine months of biological magic, Man's sperm turned out to be a depressingly simple, single-minded, multiwiggly beast. Many men have yet to recover fully from this blow to their fragile self-esteem.

The Continuing Romance of Alexander Ha and Doreen Yip, or The Phallic Fallacy

Doreen Yip declared on their honeymoon night, "I want to have a baby, but it has to be a blonde, blue-eyed girl with regular features, have a slender waist and a higher than average I.Q."

"I'll do the best I can," Alexander Yip said, unzipping his trousers.

"That's just not good enough, I'm afraid," she replied.

Alexander slowly zipped his trousers back up. He sat down on the edge of the matrimonial bed, passed a hand over his face, through his hair.

"Listen," he began, softly, patiently, "I've agreed that you are going to continue your many weekly exercise classes, that I'll cook dinner three times a week as well as vacuum and dust our bedroom and the living room, and that you'll take care of the bathroom and kitchen, and that you'll have a regular night out with the girls—I mean, women—females—your person friends—every Wednesday—but to guarantee the color of our child's hair just isn't within the realm of negotiation."

"Don't be silly. Anything's possible if you put your mind to it. Just look at ovaries."

Alexander Ha winced.

Doreen Yip offered a compromise. "I have an idea. Perhaps you could make multiple deposits to a local sperm bank and have each sample analyzed and then, when we find the right batch, I can be artificially inseminated."

"What happens if *your* genes give her kinky black hair?"

"Listen, you take care of your end, I'll take care of mine."

"But, honey." Alexander Ha cooed, trying a different tack, one with strong, philosophical roots: "Life is just not made that way—"

"It can be made that way with a little effort, determination, and force of character."

"But sweetheart. Life is chance. It's a roll of the dice—"

"That's my child you're talking about, there."

"Life's haphazard, incoherent, variable—"

Doreen Yip made a revolting sound in her throat. "Sometimes you can be *so male*."

He gave up.

"Okay, okay. Let me get this straight. You want me to go to a sperm bank, make a deposit, and then, when everything's checked out A-OK, you'll go and make a withdrawal?"

"That's right. It'll be a joint account."

"Must our relationship be quite so dehumanized?"

"What do you mean?"

"Couldn't we just make love?"

The repugnant sound once more rumbled within her throat. "Alexander, please. We live in modern times."

"Lord, don't remind me."

Alexander Ha grew despondent realizing that from here on in his penis was to be relegated to mere phallic symbol status.

Commentary

For some time now, women have been treating men as equals, which, depending on the male is either a relief or a provocation.

(or a reasonable facsimile)

Women now desire male lovers who can also be their *friends*. Now, the term *friend* used in this context can distress the average male. For him, friendship denotes trust and a certain emotional intimacy, which males are willing to give females, up to a point. To males, friendship traditionally means beers with the boys or throwing the ball for the dog to retrieve. And while it is well known that women will sometimes drink a certain amount of beer, they'll usually balk at retrieving a ball. For males, agreeing to friendship with a woman can often be a disorienting experience. She will routinely want to pour out all her thoughts, share her feelings, and then expect the male to do likewise. This horrifies the male. Nowadays, he has enough troubles without letting anyone else know.

The End of the Road for Doreen Yip and Alexander Ha, or The Friendship Bull
At the dinner table Doreen Yip began, "Alexander?"
"Yes?"
"I want a divorce but to remain friends with you afterwards."
Alexander Ha quietly put down his forkful of leathery beef with lumpy gravy he had cooked that evening. "Say what?"
"I'll repeat it if I must, but I thought–"
"*What* the *hell* did you say?"
"Now don't start getting all angry and male. You know I can't stand it when you start thriving on your testosterone."
"*Divorced!?*"
"Please. I thought we could discuss this calmly, trusting you would have a mature reaction."
"I could murder you."
"Fine. If you're going to be this way about it, I'll wait until the dessert."

"I burnt the pudding. Why in God's name do you suddenly want a divorce?" Using disassociating methods, he thrust lumps of food into this mouth and gnawed, emphatically.

"Alexander, I feel smothered. Marriage has become so stifling to my growth potential. Please don't make those animalistic sounds when I'm talking to you–I want to come to an understanding."

Chewing his food with violent, nasty grunts helped Alexander Ha sublimate his death instinct, which often arose whenever his wife insisted on having a discussion in order to arrive at an understanding.

"But first," Doreen continued, "I think you should know, above all, Alex, that you've made the last sixteen months of my life very– "

"Happy?"

"–Challenging. I respect you very much as a human being, I just don't want you as a husband."

"Doreen, you'd be respectable, too, if only you were a duck-billed platypus."

"Please don't reduce our discussion to name-calling."

"What did you expect? I've given you the best sixteen months of my life, which I'll never have back. I've given you everything you ever wanted."

"I know. Perhaps that's why our marriage failed. I merely became the instrument for your generosity. You developed a part of your identity by giving to me. Yet I felt I was becoming too much of an object to you. I felt used, and finally dissatisfied. And now I don't think our relationship works, except on the most conventional level as husband and wife. But that's just the outer trappings, which is just not enough for me. You know how I've always been much more concerned about the soul and its workings."

She paused.

(or a reasonable facsimile)

"Keep talking," Alexander said, his forehead resting on the top of the dinner table in front of him. "I'm speechless for the time being."

"Well, Alexander, I still believe we do have some things in common—"

"Hooray."

"You said you were speechless, Alexander, so do try to match word with deed. I need to get what I have to say out of my system. All right then. Now, as I tried to say, I think we certainly do have certain things in common, but not nearly enough to sustain a lifelong intimate relationship under the guise of marriage. I think, though, that as we put this part of our life behind us, we can still remain friends."

"Friends?" he echoed, lifting his head slowly from the table.

"Friends," she smiled.

"Close friends?"

"Well, I don't know whether I would go quite that far."

"Nodding acquaintances?"

"Oh. I see. You're being flippant. Why do men always do that? I was being serious, Alexander."

"You want to remain friends?"

"I just think it would be a shame if, after all the time and effort we've put in, we were to drift apart."

"You want to get divorced. Yet not drift apart."

"Alexander."

"Explain this to me: how can I be a friend to someone who rejects and divorces me?"

"I'm not rejecting you. I think it's our marriage that's to blame."

Alexander looked at his wife for a long, long moment. "And to think, sixteen months together, you've been talking to me like this all that time, and yet I really only tried to strangle you twice—"

"Can you stick to the subject for once, Alexander?"

"You stick to the subject." He got up from the dinner table. "I'm going to eat dessert."

Commentary

In summation, the state of marriage has yet to be a precise method for discovering yourself. Indeed, in the vast majority of cases, it's just considered a short-term stopgap.

In general, it is highly advisable to find oneself *before* marriage takes place, otherwise there's a pretty good chance that you'll disappear completely into the state of pseudomatrimonial bliss, and hence be lost to your true self forever. The primary mode in which this dissolution takes place is known as *Continual Compromise.* Performed often enough, compromise in marriage can lead to the odd sensation of not knowing where you end and your spouse begins. This is clearly an anti-self tactic. On the other hand, there are others who believe marriage to be just another form of long, drawn-out Death Wish.

And of course, there are all the rest who just shut up and eat their burnt pudding.

The Importance of Focus

Well, we seriously need to focus on the importance of Focus.

People who are incapable of focusing on anything for any length of time are not likely to ever find their selves. Themselves? Any who, the following conversation took place while walking along a typical city street with a microphone and a sweaty, anxious look, stopping the first person who didn't say, "Get out of my face and don't waste my time".[17]

"Hello! Excuse me?"

---

[17] This example was inserted in the book simply to illustrate an extreme case of someone who is utterly incapable of focusing on anything for any length of time and thus very likely will never, ever find himself. Herself. To show that such things do exist. That your mother isn't the only person who will never, ever know who she really is, I mean deep dark down inside. To find oneself you do need to concentrate steadily for a certain period of time, if not years. And since you appear able to read this book–after all, you've gotten this far–you should have a fairly 50/50 chance of finding yourself. You've shown gumption persisting to the point of even reading this footnote. The thing is, though, if you can read all the way through this meaningless footnote, one has to question why you haven't stopped to turn the page and got on with the rest of the book, not to say your life. Statistically speaking, this shows that either your attention span is indiscriminate, or you really have nothing better to do with your time than read the nonsense contained here instead of finding yourself or grooming a domestic pet or pitching your cheeks to make them a bright red. But hey, you paid your money, you can read every word. Every word. Every word. Meanwhile, I'm heading on over to the next chapter. Every word. You can stick around here if you want ... loser.

"Who?"
"You."
"Me?"
"Listen, may I ask whether you know who you are?"
"What? I'm sorry, what were you saying?"
"I was asking you whether you know who you are?"
"Wow. You speak fast."
"Just normal."
"Wow, really fast, man."
"How's your attention span?"
"I'm sorry. What did you say?"
"I said–"
"I'm told I got a really short attention span."
"That's what I was asking."
"What is it you wanted again?"
"What I originally said was, 'Listen, may I ask you whether you know who you are?' Remember?"
"You lost me again. I like things short."
"Short?"
"Short sentences, short movies, short books. Couldn't you break what you're saying into words?"
"What. About. Into. Syllables."
"Cool! You'd that for me?"
"Sure."
"And I won't owe you money or anything."
"No."
"Isn't life great? ...what did you want again...?"
"Listen–"
"Okay. I'm listening. That much I got."

(or a reasonable facsimile)

"I want to ask—"
"Slow down! Slow down! What's the big hurry?"
"May I—"
"You?"
"Me, yes. May I ask you something?"
"There you go again. Words, words, words."
"Okay.... May I ask whether—"
"Yeah, right, now that makes sense."
"You know yourself?"
"Me?"
"Yes."
"Okay. Fine. You've got my attention."
"Have I?"
"You want to know something."
"Yes."
"About me."
"Yes."
"What?"
"Who you are?"
"How do you mean?"
"Do you know who you are?"
"—?"
"What happened?"
"You lost me again."
"Oh. Okay. Well, thank you for your time. And have a good day."
"What are you babbling about? Hey, do I know you…? Because I. You know. I can like … Really sort of … Definitely … It's not that … More like … Sort of … Where was I? What is this? Am I? Like, wow. Yeah, well, like. Whatever."

The Implosion Theory
Dr. Maxwell P. Appleberry, PhD

> *The following is a reprint of a speech given by Dr. Maxwell P. Appleberry to the Doubters of Western Civilization Association last fall in Blandbanks, Alaska, a locale many participants did not actually believe existed until they were actually sitting in the Civic Center Auditorium and breathing the air and reading the large placard above the stage which read, "Welcome, maybe."*

Good evening, Doubters!

Implosion. I define the act of imploding as a more or less total collapse inward. When applying this concept to the act of searching for one's self, things become one heck of a lot more messy.

Today I will address the implications of the implosion theory in daily life. And if time permits, I'd like to cover it week by week as well.

However, I am fully cognizant that there will be a number of you in the audience who will tend to doubt the validity of what

I'm about to present, but that's to be expected; for I'm given to understand that the majority of you in the audience today consider Doubt a full-time hobby, and/or replacement for the sexual instinct—

(*Here the speaker was interrupted by booing from the audience.*)

Be that as it may, I shall continue.
(*More boos.*)

I'm pleased to say that, over-all, the Implosion Theory leaves little room for doubt—although I'm certain you'll find that little room—as to whether or not it is a substantial contribution to the science of the mind, and whether its theoretical framework is satisfactory in its consanguinity to other well-established modern fundamental principles and/or hypotheses and/or this one and that one. To which I can only emphatically answer, well, of course.

Its primary benefit is in the search for self. Beyond any doubt.
(*A few mumbled protests heard from the audience.*)

I prefer to tackle the elucidation of my theory in the form of question and answer. There remain reoccurring anxieties as to my theory with which I frequently come into contact, either via the mail or by direct physical confrontation, usually after my talks. People who want to explode rather than implode come up to me with fists tightened to debate implosion. Obviously, they haven't understood a single word. So I hope everyone here will make a teensy effort at understanding, because I'm getting tired of people taking swings at me.

Question: My husband thinks I'm losing my mind because I sing when he attempts to kiss me. Is he right?
Answer: Partly, but not categorically. Many women, after years of marriage, often have the urge to sing when they see their

(or a reasonable facsimile)

husbands preparing to lay a kiss on them. The woman, in fact, would truly like to scream, but she's uncertain as to how her husband of many years would take this. She's afraid he would not understand, which would be understandable, depending on the song.

But this phenomenon surprisingly offers a clear example as to how the implosion theory operates.

Now, I ask that you follow the implosion workings closely here. Wife views husband's lips puckering. No need for alarm from the wife as yet, merely the first flickers of concern. But then the lips turn toward her. Alarm activated. A scream of tension wells up—but they are married, and Society possesses a conservative attitude on the kissing rituals of the married couple; plus she is aware of the basic outlines of mental health and its normal manifestations. She wants to scream, but she also wants to avoid being accused of having faulty mental circuits and declared a wacko, so she does not scream.

Yet the vocal energy is on the rise. It cannot be denied. She panics, she implodes. She sings. She changes the god-awful shriek of horror to a melodic note just in time. She breaks into a brief operatic aria. The husband is miffed, the woman is relieved, tension and art have mingled and another marriage saved thanks to the implosion mechanism.

Question: If so, how come?
Answer: This is true, and deserves especial attention, if not elaboration. Many people, it has come to my attention, lend no credence at all to my implosion theory; indeed, some are under the impression that I'm on a wild goose chase and

just making all this up as I go along. The explanation for these reactions is relatively simple. Many people, the same ones in fact, are not even aware that the implosion theory exists. This explains much. It explains neglect. It reveals dreadful educational lapses. Even, sometimes, it unveils naked women who should know better. But be that as it may, as it so often is, according to my experience, which is extensive, though by no means all inclusive, although my life's work is moving toward that objective, I find I have lost my way in his sentence and must begin this answer all over again.

Oh, let me fetch up another question instead.

Question: Is there a God?

Answer: A very interesting question. And succinctly put. Although a great deal of strenuous imploding must occur before a final decision can be arrived at in this particular instance. I would like to reserve my absolute and final conclusion on this one until more extensive imploding experiences are researched, recorded, and the general tendencies studied. We do have a few preliminary graphs and sliding scales in the development stage, some of which face the Jesus Christ Question straight on, with suspicious, sidelong glances at the Buddha, Mohammed, and the Greek Goddess disputes. But as yet, God has proven somewhat elusive, imploded or not. We're hopeful, though.

Question. Is it good to doubt? Or evil?

Answer: At this point in my presentation, I wish to assure everyone gathered here that these questions are quite legitimate. I am not making them up merely to provoke or antagonize the Doubters Association gathered here today. I really do

(or a reasonable facsimile)

have the piece of paper that was collected at the beginning of this conference and has been contained in a previously sealed envelope until this instant.
(*Waves it in the air for the audience to see.*)

But to face the question of good and evil in doubt. The implosion theory is fairly adamant on this. Doubt is a natural human attribute to the pre-imploded individual. Once, however, mental implosion has occurred, doubt is cured of its seductive charms.

Please believe me, I would never think of categorically stating that doubt possesses certain stigmas, or that it should be outlawed, or have amendments to many countries' constitutions introduced and its banishment actively lobbied for—no, I would not go quite that far. I would, however, approach this territory.
(*Here again, the speaker is interrupted by boos and catcalls, some of an obscene nature.*)

You refuse to understand! Make an effort! The implosion theory states quite clearly that, as a shortcut to self-knowledge, my theory has proven beneficial, relatively benign, and even fun if you're doing it with someone else who's even more befuddled than you. It cannot maim, and the spontaneous sterilization rate is low. And no one has yet attempted suicide with the implosion technique, although we did hear about one funny guy last month who tried some macabre stuff with some cadavers and a pogo stick. But one is bound to run into such isolated incidents when making major breakthroughs.

So, to return to doubt–
(*A rising hostility is heard throughout the crowd.*)

Stop this noise! I shall not continue if this abuse does not cease immediately.
(*Cheers.*)
Now stop that. Right this minute. Shame, shame! I was optimistic that this convention and its semi-distinguished members might have a slightly more open attitude to divergent opinions. Evidently, I was misinformed.

And to think, you are all expert doubters, and yet here you sit, without a doubt, so sure and smug in your disapproval of me and my implosion theory.
(*The audience quiets markedly.*)
Ah! That hit home. So, my dubious doubters, may I return to the questions at hand...? Hmm, thanks to your interruption, I have forgotten the question. I'll pick another one.

Question: What is your favorite color? And what's your favorite food?
Answer: Blue. And pizza.

Question: My mother and father were awful. I had a terrible childhood. My life has been a series of failures, both personal and professional. The doctors think I have the first signs of an incurable illness. Can implosion help?
Answer: Well, let's not get too carried away with my implosion theory. It *has* had certain salutary effects; the general outlook is positive; but as yet I'd be extremely cautious as to offer it as a cure-all. Especially to really screwed up people. So far, it's worked best with upper-middle-class people with very few personal problems or material worries. But that does not necessarily mean that my theory is limited in scope; it simply means all the results are not

(or a reasonable facsimile)

yet in.

    I'd like to add, though, that if this person is still alive in five years time, I'll have more data to pass along that may be of use. I appreciate the question and sympathize. In the meanwhile, hang in there.

Question: Dear Doctor, I just today realized that my feet sweat whenever I get close to another human being. My hands get red welts when I stroke my little doggie. My lips twitch when I see a cat. Kangaroos strike me as obscene yet possums are bearable. I tend to drool a little—very little—hardly at all, really—when in a stuffy room, and yet when I'm frozen stiff I can't stop cutting farts. My husband indulges me and accepts my peculiarities with a noble stoicism—I just wish he'd talk to me more often. My daughter, on the other hand, refuses to invite her friends over to the house for cookies and milk. And I don't care if she's twenty-three and working on her master's degree, I'd like to meet her friends. And then, of course, yes, there are caterpillars—

Answer: Enough. I know trick questions when I see them.

(*He is booed off stage, doubtfully.*)

Warning:
The Dangers of Not Finding Yourself

Believe it or not, there live and breathe, reproduce and consume natural resources, a tiny, tiny, tiny minority—I mean really small—an inconsequential cult almost—of retrograde entities who steadfastly, even belligerently, assert that the Self is no big deal. That the search is itself a delusion. That authors of How to Find Yourself handbooks should find a steady job or have their testicles removed.

Well, such attitudes have consequences.

As examples scream louder than puffed-up, thick-dictioned, revenge-seeking academic prose, we were able to nab right off the street one of these aggressive humanoids called Sam FakeNameSoYouDon'tReallyKnowWhoI'mTalkingAbout Smith, who did not believe for a single moment in the value of finding oneself.

Naturally, in order to ensure absolute partiality, the manipulative interview was performed in the most antiseptic, scientific conditions possible: the subject was locked in a solid white experimental chamber, seated in a solitary white chair right in the middle of the room where I could observe him from behind a one-way mirror, communicating via an intercom.

Me: Mr. Smith?

Smith: (*startled, looking round*) Who are you? I don't like this room at all. Where am I?

Me: Now why do you think you feel particularly anxious sitting in a large, empty, completely white room with no way out?

Smith: (*unsolicited sarcasm*) Gee, *I don't know*. Total sensory deprivation in a blank room. Explain to me why I'm here again?

Me: You are a research specimen for an ongoing monograph on the art and science of self-realization. After analyzing what I'm about to find out about you, the information will be placed in a subsection on belligerent resistance to self.

Smith: (*making a small laugh*) You want to play a few games with me.

Me: Let's start with something simple you can handle. Tell us about yourself.

Smith: Right. I was born into a no-nonsense, Mid-Western family of hard-working farmers, proud of their sweat, their brow, and proud of the land they cultivated. A thoroughly industrious, self-reliant clan, not given to asking themselves *why* this and *why* that–couldn't imagine my uncle Clem, red-necked and callused hands, picking an ear of corn and wondering, What is the meaning of it all?

Me: What I'm hearing is that your family, as a whole, was resistant to the process of psychological self-examination?

Smith: Man, I can tell you never reaped what you sowed. You use way too many syllables in your words to be in touch with a working man's reality.

Me: There are other states to touch on than that of toil and soil.

Smith: At least what we touch, we feel. You ever touch this Self

(or a reasonable facsimile)

stuff? Run it through your fingers? Measure it on a weight machine? I don't see the point of having to go fingering your Self all the time—you do life and the rest'll take care of itself. Like vegetables, wheat, staples.
Me: There exist certain individuals who wouldn't be in accord with you.
Smith: Oh yeah? Such as?

(*At this point a male from New York City of Jewish extraction was introduced with a sudden pop into Smith's environment.*)

New Yorker: Oy! Vhat am I doink here?
Me: You are in an all white room with a complete stranger. Can't you see that?
New Yorker: I can *see* that, but it doesn't necessarily make it true.
Smith: (*very suspicious*) Say, who are ya, fella?
New Yorker: I'm a neurotic racial stereotype. Very high-strung. And they've taken away my medication from me for the last two days.
Smith: Who let you in here?
New Yorker: A large, dominating woman, like my mother. She even had dark fuzz on her upper lip, like my mother. I was repulsed and captivated at the same time. I wanted to hit her and hug her. Alternatively. Like with mother.
Smith: (*backing away warily*) How d'you mean, alternatively? Like every other day?
New Yorker: No! (*growing shrill*) Every other minute. Hit – hug – hit – hug – hit – hug!
Smith: You just stay right on your side of the room there, bud.
New Yorker: Bud? My name's David L. Stein, I'm circumcised, hate chicken soup, and want to sleep with my mama. Help me!
Smith: (*whispering urgently to the walls*) Get him out of here, scientist guy. (*to Stein*) And you stay over there, bud.

How to Find Yourself

New Yorker: Again, rejection! Rejection!!! Do you have any idea what it's like to be me?
Smith: Stop your whimpering, be a man—

(*At this point, Stein is abruptly removed, also with a pop.*)

Me: Well, reactions?
Smith: (clearly shaken, returning to the center of the room and chair) Was that one of your successful cases? (sits back down, slowly)
Me: Let me correct an apparent misapprehension on your part. I am in no way a doctor or a therapist. I am an investigator into the psychological phenomenon of humankind.
Smith: All those syllables. Is making with the words part of the so-called knowing of the Self? I'm me and blah blah blah forever? Huh? Answer me? Am I right or am I right? Well?

(*The subject was left to fidget in an uncomfortable silence for eight minutes.*)

Smith: Why don't you say something? Is this part of whatever you're doing? The scientific test stuff? (*Waits for an answer*) Hello?

(*More psychologically inflected silence.*)

Smith: (*oddly subdued*) Is it over then? Can I go home?
Me: *NO!* (*Subject jumps in chair*) I must now open my investigation into your skepticism to include random association. I'll say something and you tell me the first thing that comes to your mind.
Smith: Purple asparagus tips.
Me: I haven't started yet.
Smith: Sorry, but that's the first thing that always springs to mind when I'm left on my own. Are you going to write that down and

(or a reasonable facsimile)

tell me what that means?
Me: Shut-up!
Smith: Now just a minute there, bud–
Me: Purple asparagus tips.
Smith: That's mine!
Me: Tell me the first word or image that comes into your mind!
Smith: Oh. We're starting then?
Me: Yes, yes, yes. Please respond! Purple asparagus tips.
Smith: My mother on her death bed.
Me: A gingerbread cake made with the wrong recipe.
Smith: My father leading me to the shed to give me a whipping. I'm five years old.
Me: A circumcised male New Yorker.
Smith: My ma and pa grunting and connected near the new dug well in broad daylight and me and my sis locked in the cellar because they said a twister was on its way. They … lied.

(*Here the subject's anxiety level increased markedly; he exhibited the classic tendency to place one index finger in one ear and, by applying a constant pressure, push it through his head and out the other ear while grinning sheepishly.*)

Me: Peanut butter and jelly.
Smith: (*in a burst*) Gopher holes! (*he sobbed*)
Me: Upright nipples.
Smith: (*now pulling absentmindedly at his tongue while humming Beethoven's Fifth Symphony in B-Flat*) My father's boots. Big, huge, enormous.
Me: Red strawberries.
Smith: (*toppling on the floor*) My mother's womb!
Me: Curds and whey?
Smith: My father's womb!

85

How to Find Yourself

Me: Bacons and eggs and a side order of coffee!
Smith: Gaa-gaa, goo-goo...

Here the subject reverted to the prenatal position, and was handed over to the proper psychiatric authorities.

This goes to prove that even the most hardened, skeptical, aggressive, Mid-Western corn-picker can be driven to the extremes of his most inner being where there's hardly any light to see by, given the proper scientific conditions and some really hostile badgering.

Any questions?

Finding Your Own Voice

Try humming.[18]

---

[18] Or, if you're a man, place your testicles on a low table and tap them oh so lightly with a ball-peen hammer. Listen to the resultant noise you make deep in the back of your throat. Is that *really* you back there? Is that the voice that says *you?* Or, if you're a woman, pinch your nipples really, really hard until you cry out. Of course, if you are a masochist, *don't* pinch your nipples for three days until you scream. And there your voice will be, either one or the other. (If only everything was this simple.)

Madness and a Sense of Self
Case Study

Sally Simpson was an unusual patient. She was young, intelligent, and beautiful, but had an unfortunate fixation on madness. She was not mad. She merely liked the idea of it.

She appeared at our clinic's reception desk early one morning in Spring.

"Hello."

"Hello."

Initial signs pointed to a personality adapted to normal social interaction.

She asked, "Is this 111111 Really Healthy Street?"

"Yes," responded our capable receptionist.

"The Self-Realization, Actualization, Detonation Center?"

"Yes."

"*The* Self-Realization, Actualization, Detonation Center?"

"Yes. Why?"

"Good. I want to check in."

"Check in?"

"Yes."

"But this is not a hotel," our receptionist explained. "You have to be mentally ill or very wealthy to check in here."

"Oh. well, I don't have all that much money, but I'm a bit nuts."

"Are you sure? You seem normal."

"Well, it's more like I want to go mad, but I need someplace safe to do it."

"I see. One moment, please."

I was summoned.

"Yes?" I asked, examining this young person's body language as I approached. I noted the loose way her arms hung by her sides, the quizzical way her cocked her head to one side, her fine, firm figure. There was no immediate necessity for calling the armed security guards. "I'm a doctor," I said. "May I help you?"

"I certainly hope so," she replied. "I want to go mad. Can you help me?"

"*Help* you go mad, do you mean?"

"Yeah, really crazy."

"I'm sorry, but this is a purely curative institution. You see, we help people *out* of the state of madness; we do not knowingly induce the symptoms."

"Oh." She looked crestfallen. "That's too bad. You see, I'm pretty normal for my age group and sex, but it's kinda boring, if you know what I mean. I sort of wanted to try out madness for a while. See what it's like. And if it was sort of cool, then apply for permanent status, or at least permission for extension."

"I'm sorry, Miss–?"

"Simpson. Sally Simpson."

"I regret, Miss Simpson, but what you request is totally out of the question."

(or a reasonable facsimile)

"I've got some money. It's not a lot, but I've been saving for months. Please."

"Out of the question. It's unethical. Immoral. Plus, I've never done it before."

"How about something sort of *like* madness, then? Acute schizophrenia?"

I shook my head.

"Mild psychosis?"

"No."

"Temporary catatonia?"

"Absolutely not."

"Bed-wetting? *Some*thing. Come on, give me a break."

"I'm sorry, but you're under some sort of misapprehension—"

"Enough to get me committed?" she asked eagerly.

"I'm afraid not."

Again, she looked crestfallen. "Okay. But can you at least give me an address where they might take me? Maybe I could be a scientific paper and appear in a prestigious journal as a case study, or something...."

I was about to dismiss her and get back to my real work when this singular idea suddenly gave me a different, daring idea.

"Well ... if you'll leave your telephone number where I can contact you, Miss Simpson, I'll see what I can do."

"Oh goody!" she cried, jumping up and down.

Generally speaking, in my profession, I only receive the messy end result of mental disease; those remanded into my care have usually reached the far edge of their own distorted universe unaided; I have had no hand in the matter. The case had never before arisen where I could actually take a perfectly normal human specimen and watch mental deterioration set in.

Thus I admit I was intrigued by Miss Simpson's request, but purely on scientific grounds. I had had some theoretical experiments forming in the back of my mind for some while, calling for a mentally fit subject. Radical experiments which would be necessary in completing the lecture I was due to deliver that summer to a group of Radical Psychologists in Stockholm, entitled, *Madness, what it is, what it isn't, who's got it, who hasn't*, or, *Madness and a Sense of Self*–and now Miss Sally Simpson had appeared, apparently volunteering her mental health for the advancement of science. She was young, of a pleasant disposition, cheerful and harmless, and just a shade peculiar. Perfect for a test case.

I organized and readied my experiments, extending an invitation to Sally Simpson via telephone.

"Great!" she responded joyfully. "Tests! If I pass them, do I get to go nuts?"

"I'm not promising anything," I cautioned.

"Hey, I know you'll do your best. I've been reading some of your books and articles I found. Hey, you're kinda weird, too, aren't ya? But I guess you have to be bit off-center to be drawn to madness in the first place. That's why I'm attracted to madness–being mad is pretty weird generally, right?"

"It has its facets."

"I bet it does. Hey, shall I bring an overnight bag, or what? How long are you gonna let me be mad?"

I informed her we would require between two days and eight weeks, but that a lot depended on her susceptibility to mental derangement, and that I could still not promise anything. Also, that she would be required to sign several legal documents and release forms. She cheerfully agreed to everything, giggling delightfully over the phone.

(or a reasonable facsimile)

Sally Simpson was an even-tempered, twenty-six-year-old ex-medical student ("I've always had a thing for illness"), stood 5'6" in her stocking feet, but refused to remove any further clothing until she felt properly insane and unable to control her bodily functions.

"Geez, just talking about loosing control sends chills up and down my spine. I mean, like, complete and total mental derangement, how cool."

All vital signs were tested and proved positive. We commenced bright and early the first day.

Day One
Doctor: Your name?
Patient: Sally Simpson.
Doctor: Will you go to bed with me and have wild, meaningless sex?
Patient: I'm still rational, doc – so no deal.
The first day's tests were unsatisfactorily concluded.

Day Two
Doctor: Please, say the first word that comes to mind.
Patient: Okay.
Doctor: Left.
Patient: Right.
Doctor: Front.
Patient: Back.
Doctor: Up.
Patient: Down.
Doctor: Tell me, how long have you had this neurotic compulsion toward fool-proof logic?
Patient: (crestfallen) Ever since I was taught that it was the normal way to think. I'm a hopeless case, aren't I? Plain and normal,

mentally healthy – how boring. Isn't there any hope?

Doctor: Have patience.

Patient: But I've been patient all my life. Nothing interesting ever happens to me. I have a father who's a psychologist, and a mother who's a social worker. They were always being extra special careful not to do anything to me that might cause neurosis. No loud orders or abrupt moods. And when I wanted to talk, they always made time to listen. It was awful. I don't know why I just didn't go mad naturally, without having to seek your help. My parents constructed a perfectly wholesome environment for me to grow up in, made me socially well adjusted, pleasant, intelligent, bland.... Then one day I confronted them with all this. (The patient grew emotional.) I accused them. I reproached them! I told them how they had failed! Utterly! And you know what they said? They understood! They told me my reactions were all very normal and healthy. I told them I hated their guts and wished they were dead and they replied it was just a phase I was going through but that they appreciated my honesty. (The patient began calming down.) But ... but hey, don't think I want to go crazy just to prove something to them. No. I've analyzed my motivations, doc. I want to experience insanity so as to know what's at the depths of my being.

Doctor: Perfectly normal.

Patient: Oh God, now you sound just like my Dad!

Doctor: Pardon me.

Patient: It's okay. But you see what I'm getting at? I want to know myself in an extreme situation before it's too late. I'm young, I have no ties, so before I settle down, I want to have an idea of absolute raving lunacy so in the future I

(or a reasonable facsimile)

won't look back and feel I missed out on something when I was young, and then regret it.
Doctor: Do you have any particular role models in mind?
Patient: You mean mad folks I look up to? No, not really. I have no ideal where being nuts is concerned. I'll just take whatever I can get.
Doctor: If we may continue the tests now...?

The patient Sally Simpson was given an exhaustive battery of manual, spatial, and psychic coordination and organization skills tests for the subsequent fourteen hours. She proved abnormally normal and proficient at each skill, except for the one calling for sexual abandonment and copulation with the physician in charge ("First wacko, doc – a deal's a deal," was how the patient phrased it.).

As a further experiment and aid toward development of the desired mental derangement, I informed the patient that her results to date were excellent and above board, and that she was an exceedingly well-adjusted taxpayer, but that if she continued in this manner I would have no recourse but to discharge her with a clean bill of mental health. Interestingly, she appeared despondent.

Day Three
Doctor: How are you today?
Patient: (no response)
Doctor: Aren't you feeling well?
Patient: (no response)
Doctor: Will you go to bed with me?
Patient: (no response)
Doctor: Excellent. I think we're finally beginning to make some progress.

The patient had fallen into a severe depression overnight. After bedtime, the attending nurse reported overhearing the patient having violent nightmares and murmuring, "I know I'm perfectly normal, but that doesn't mean I'm a bad person."

Day Four
The following day, the patient's outward responses were minimal; most aural stimulation had no effect; visual stimulation also proved ineffectual; only when I scientifically applied my fingertips gently to her cheekbones and moved them in playful circular motions did the patient respond with a faint sneer: evidently, she did not consider her self so far gone as to warrant unfettered examination.

In order to induce a further retreat from reality and increase the level of self-absorption and self-pity, I warned the patient that if she continued in her present condition, I'd summon her parents to witness how she had failed at insanity, and thus instinctively obeying her parents highly normal upbringing.

Gratifyingly, the patient withdrew further, soon slipping noiselessly out of her chair and collapsing in a heap on the floor. Orderlies were summoned. They carried her to her new private chamber in the intensive mental care ward.

Nurses were given strict instructions to repeat to the patient every fifteen minutes for the next twenty-four hours the unvarying phrase, "Your parents are very proud of you, and they are coming to give you a big, big hug, you perfectly normal child."

I was, of course, extremely curious and hopeful as to the end result.

(or a reasonable facsimile)

Day Five
The last day of experiments took place bedside.
The Patient, drawn and pale, stared at the ceiling without blinking, muttering, "Kung Fu is my middle name."
Without preliminary verbal exchange, I dove straight into the final series of madness testing and began fondling her anatomy, at first with caution, then with increasing vigor. The patient did not respond. I took this development as a good sign. I then invited various interns into the room. We played ping-pong on her belly. We put on silly masks and made funny sounds. Once in a while I threw in some experimental fondling for good measure. The patient at no time showed any flicker of interest. I then deemed it prudent to conclude with the last experiment, which, due to the nature of my classified methods, I am unable to reveal here at this time. I can only relate that it consisted of the usual manifestations of strenuous scientific inquiry. And that upon completion, the gathered interns applauded.

Conclusion
Sally Simpson was certified insane the following day. Her parents were contacted and arrived at the clinic with their lawyers. They were then shown the signed and witnessed legal forms. Their daughter was turned over to them, as state law demands.
Twenty-five months later, after unremitting care and therapy at another rival clinic across town, Sally Simpson was returned to a certified state of normalcy.
The patient has communicated her gratitude to our Center with the following letter:

> Dear Doctor and All My Friends at the Clinic,
> I want to express my deepest gratitude to the Center for its

time and energy. I have framed my Certificate of Insanity. I will always recall you with great fondness.

I am now married, have two children, and reside far, far away. But let us exchange Christmas cards annually.

Yours with fondest memories,
SS

Editor's Note

Although madness in this particular case aided Sally Simpson to a surer self-knowledge and a degree of contentment, out-and-out looniness cannot as yet be recommended to the general reader as a foolproof route to finding oneself. Indeed, madness in the vast majority of cases is looked upon as a severe setback in mental health.

Thus, the reader is urged to consult other portions of this book for aid in seeking one's inner self, and only turning to madness as a last, and admittedly risky, resort.

Schizophrenia and You

As the attentive reader may have noted by now, there seems to be a curious reccurrence–a certain blurred relationship–between finding oneself and being out of your mind. This does not mean that one necessarily follows the other, or even vice versa, yet this phenomenon has made itself all too manifest a bit too often in some of the accounts reported in these pages. Why madness should have such a significant part in the search for Self is not yet clear; yet rest assured; we're busy studying it. Some of the more talented minds have yet to crack the dilemma, while some of the lesser-talented minds tend to become the dilemma.

But let's take a quick look here:
- The symptoms of schizophrenia often include hallucinations, delusions, paranoia and disembodied voices.
- Does one encounter such goings-on in the search for Self?
- Well, yes and no.
- In schizophrenia, the afflicted confuses fantasy with reality.
- In finding oneself, the afflicted confuses oneself with reality.
- Some experts contend there is no difference.

- Some experts insist there are great differences.

And there you have it in a nutshell. As long as you have more than two people on earth, you'll have disagreements ... Of an almost schizophrenic nature.

Further comparisons:
- Schizophrenia, once it strikes, lasts a lifetime.
- Once one has found oneself, one usually remains like that for the rest of one's life.

So, yes, it cannot be denied, there are points of comparison.

Opposing this, schizophrenics deteriorate gradually but inevitably; while, generally speaking, those who find themselves feel better and better (and if you *don't*, then maybe you are way out of your skull, and in that case, I really can't help you[19]).

---

[19] Really.

Inner Peace and a Sense of Self

Upon the discovery of your own true self, a normal expectation is that serenity and inner peace should be forthcoming.

Well, you would think.

However, this outcome cannot be fully guaranteed.[20]

To cover this subject to ensure readers get their money's worth, follow-up inquiries were made on those who had found themselves, asking them how they felt, post-their-true-selves. Many responses of an inarticulate nature jammed my letterbox, email and several hours of my answering machine.[21] Those fully satisfied with being themselves tended not to reply, due, no doubt, to their being too pleased with themselves to answer unsolicited requests for their time.

Included below are some of the more articulate, less obscene replies.

---

[20] See just about any other section of this book.

[21] The most common reply I received (besides death threats) was, and I quote: "Life's just a lot better now.... It's really sorta hard to explain. To put into words, I mean. You sort of had to have been me, before *and* after, if you know what I mean, to know what I mean. Does that make sense?"

Melanie White, school teacher

I had always been vaguely dissatisfied with myself. Ever since adolescence there had been a sense of incompletion hanging over me, as though there should have been more me than there was.

I taught kindergarten for much of my adult life and it wasn't very character building or personally demanding—teaching finger painting day-in, day-out, is not really a sure path to inner knowledge.

Then one day, while leafing through a clothes and furniture catalog I'd gotten through the mail because my name was on some mailing list and I just kept receiving this junk and out of habit looked through it all, and afterwards stacking the catalogs neatly in my closet, never throwing anything away either, but never buying anything, keeping it just in case, because you never know, and yet, this time, because of what I read in this catalog, I was forcibly reminded that I didn't really know who I was. It had been so very long since I'd thought about myself I'd forgotten I'd had one, a self, that is, which I think is probably the case for a great many people.[22]

Anyway.

In this catalog I came upon one of those short quizzes you see so often and think are so silly but you go over it in your head anyhow because that's human nature. These quizzes usually ask all sorts of personal questions that tell you a great deal about yourself or the man you love. This one was different: it had three short questions, and said if you knew the answers, you were all right as a human being and a person.

The questions were—and I remember them as though it were yesterday, although it's been what, ten, fifteen years?

---
[22] See just about any chapter in this book reinforcing this impression.

(or a reasonable facsimile)

1. Who are You?
2. Are you Happy?
3. What's your birth date? (*optional*)

And do you know, I couldn't answer a single one? Even my birthday! I'd drifted so far away from the center of my being that I'd forgotten my own birthday for the last three years! No wonder life had seemed to be flowing by without meaning or significant event.

Right there and then I vowed not to look up my date of my birth until I found myself—it would be a reward—and suddenly it became an overwhelming *need* to have a birthday!

I was motivated. After so many years, it was a strange feeling, being motivated, let me tell you.

So, I worked at me. I asked questions—and I mean *lots* of questions, two dozen tons of them, at least. I read books. I went to seminars. Underwent three kinds of psychotherapy, took extra philosophy courses at night. ...I mean, it was an effort. Years of effort. But in the end, it paid off.

About four and a half years ago, I found myself and things have been quiet and settled ever since—although I must admit I was shocked to find out how old I'd become.

I teach first grade now. I've divorced my husband and married one of my former pupils who popped up one day, years after graduating from my kindergarten class, to tell me how much he appreciated my finger painting teaching, thanking me for encouraging him in an artistic direction, and that I'd had a significant influence on all his future life choices. It was sweet to hear that. He's an assistant to the Art Director of a large direct mail agency. Eric's a dear. (He still practices finger painting, although *I* am his canvas now; but that's none of your business.)

Anyway, if the truth be told, I'm fifty-something now, and can't help feeling a little melancholy as I look back at all those years I spent in the pursuit of me. The most productive years of my life. Sometimes I dream of having spent that time differently, and to have something more to show for those missing years than a peaceful inner being.

I don't know. Sometimes I could burst out crying. People say I'm having a mid-life crisis. How can I? I know who I am, don't I? But dammit, if I *am* having a mid-life crisis, I'm going to be angry. I just don't have that much time left to waste.

Oh God, I wonder how long *this* crisis is going to take....

Mike Grange, automobile mechanic
It's hell now, just pure hell. Ever since I found myself, I see things differently and it's not particularly fun. It's a whole new orientation. I sort of liked the way I saw things before, *before* I found myself. God, life, and me were a lot simpler then. When I didn't have a clue as to who my real self was, I was pretty glad to just be living and sticking my hands in some nuts and bolts, proud when a motor purred. And after work, it was TV, beer, Sunday football games, the basics. It was a pretty good life.

Then I had to go and find myself.

And I discover I should've been a lawyer all this time. *Jesus*....

So now I'm attending night school, acquiring sophisticated tastes, learning big words, manipulating logical thought and instinctively looking for loopholes. I go to foreign films and like brandy. I *read*. Big books with small print. Front to back, even the footnotes. I'm hooked. It's depressing.

But I just don't know if it's all worth it—really. This Self stuff. I've got all these new ambitions and worries. Career goals and financial liabilities. It's tough. I wouldn't recommend a true sense of self

(or a reasonable facsimile)

to anyone who's been fooling himself for years and has already gotten used to who he thinks he is and has his habits, a beer belly, a life....

Maybe if I had discovered myself earlier, before I had all these pleasant memories when I didn't know who I really was but was having a good time anyway.

My old friends really think I'm crazy now. They say, "Come on, Mike, you're crazy. Stop going to college. My carburetor's starting to go on the blink." But I explain to these people, "This is the real me, since I found myself." They back off as though I've gone loony.

Who knows. Maybe they're right.

Nowadays, I just try to keep me to myself, stop having these urges to bill people for my time, and suffer in silence....

Molly Le Georgé, an extremely rich woman
Money isn't everything—I think everyone should know that, and take it to heart. Yes, I have a lot, and I mean *a lot* of money, but it's not everything, and who should know better than I?

Rude people sometimes dare tell me I talk too much and in clichés, but I don't pay attention. Some clichés just happen to be true; it's just that if you say them too often they sound dumb. And then people assume *you're* dumb. But you're not dumb. You're simply stating the truth as plainly as you can. And that's not dumb. Well, hardy ever. I can say all this without blushing because I've found myself.

I've discovered my real essence. The real me. My inner being. And what's that? my golfing chums ask. Oh, everything. Just everything. And that's the truth. Even if people whisper behind my back that I'm banal. If it's the real me, who cares! It's *my* contentment in existence that is important—me! Not their opinion of who I am. I mean this. Profoundly.

I mean everything I say, and it's only through the grace of my newly acquired identity that I can say this. Otherwise, I wouldn't know *what* to say. Can you imagine? Before, not knowing me, I didn't know what to say, so I often said anything, anything that came into my head, I could rattle on and on, for hours, not saying anything of real interest, but now, now that I've found my soul, my inner core, I know exactly what I'm saying, I weigh every word—well, nearly every word—and I don't care what anyone else thinks. I'm secure. Only it gets on my nerves. Those people who can't comprehend my new inner wisdom. So that's one minor drawback to deep self-knowledge: people who haven't found themselves refuse to listen to me—they think they *know* better—oh, if only they really knew....

And I still insist money isn't everything.

And I don't care if you think I'm talking silly stuff and nonsense. It doesn't matter. I don't care. I don't, I don't, I don't. So there.

So, to sum up.

It appears that while some people are more temperamentally suited to handling the stressful end result of self-discovery, others, being more highly strung or of a gloomy nature, do not take so readily to a discovery of self. There are no general character traits that would inform the self-seeker whether or not he or she is temperamentally suited to the role of knowing him/herself. Sorry. However, it appears that some individuals can happily do without a real sense of self. Often, in fact, bliss, in the modern mammal, is not necessarily detected in the person who has found himself, but rather in the person who is still somebody else.

How to Buy Yourself

Dear Shopper!
For those too-busy sorts who claim they simply don't have enough time to find themselves, there is a shortcut available that takes hardly any effort at all, just a sizable bank account.

It is a concept based not so much on "Shop till you drop", as, "Shop till you're the you you're comfortable with."

The process is fairly uncomplicated. First, look in the telephone book under Merchandising Outlets. Find our local franchise of the "Buy You" emporium that are springing up everywhere and get in your car or use public transport or employ a bicycle, and get yourself over to our showroom now.

The original purpose in founding the "Buy You" emporiums was to fill a market niche and serve customers' needs. "Buy You" started small. Some T-shirts with simple, positive slogans blasted across the front and back. These were the same slogans we used in our advertising campaigns and hung on the walls of our originally called Selfee Shoppe (which market studies revealed that people thought we sounded like 'Selfish Shoppee', which in certain areas could give us a semi-negative image, whereas in other areas it increased significantly our moola factor). At that time, we also experimented with some in-shop displays of self-help books with amusing titles and huge ambitions, which brought in the public. We quickly expanded to desktop calendars with "I'm-me" reinforcing phrases for each day of the year, as well as some small vanity mirrors, an extra shelf here, a rack there, then bigger mirrors for more positive self-reinforcement, and now, this month, we're opening our 100th store in North America, and plan to expand into the Far East and Europe next year. Whether they like it or not.

Yes, "Buy You" emporiums are springing up everywhere, and we here at "Buy You" say: Stand up, show the world who you are, even if they don't want to know. *Especially* if they don't want to know.

Now, being you can be a no-hassle proposition. We have created a cozy store atmosphere enabling you to try on different personalities until whatever you you find in our stock makes you feel good.

At "Buy You," we have just the person for sale for whatever person you want to be. The vast majority of alarming existential questions may be answered and stilled by our rows and shelves and endless personality types and character traits. "Buy You" has dedicated itself to offering every possible kind of you available on the marketplace at reasonable prices. Come see for yourself (or whatever bit of self you currently have inside you at present): you'll be amazed—overwhelmed!—by our choice of outward identities.

In fact, if you are not utterly bewildered when you've been in our store for ten minutes from the sheer aggression of our merchandise abundance, or even if you've brought your own bewilderment with you, we can guarantee you a brand new person before you leave our premises, making a newly calm and self-confident you with a

(or a reasonable facsimile)

money back guarantee.[23]

If you have big feet and a big personality to match, we have the shoes to match. Our slogan for our Special Shoe Section is: "Practical shoe-wear for the truly grounded person."

And believe me, you can't find better value for self at any competing store. We here at "Buy You" are so confident of our merchandise and the sense of emphatic self-being we can generate that we guarantee to match any competitor's price, sometimes offering two snug-fit personalities for the price of one. We will not be outdone.[24]

Do you really need more proof of our offerings and value?

We have an abundant selection of hairpieces for those who believe self is to be found in the hirsute. *The more hair, the more you*, as we like to say down here at "Buy You."

We have *I am me* lipstick and *Inner Being* earrings. They come in all sorts of the latest, scientifically analyzed colors: Me Maroon, Blue Being, Identity Indigo, Saffron Self. Our most upbeat color is the exclusive, "Yellow Yourself Happy!"

Try our Insight EyeWear. Our slogan is: "See out from your inner being."

We continue to carry a wide range of our original custom-made and trademark T-shirts for those needy people going through self-confidence crises in Who They Are. Positive reinforcement is our motto down here at "Buy You." Wear T-shirts that boldly

---

[23] Guarantees can only be made to those persons purchasing "BUY YOU" products at that moment; people who return as someone else or with a modified sense of self cannot be offered exchanges or refunded money, as legally we can only deal with the personality (or lack thereof) who made the original purchase.

[24] Ignore any low-lying, dirty rotten competitor who dares try to practice cut-throat capitalism better than us and bites into our profit margin, the dirty, filthy rats. Our advice down here at "Buy You" is: Never trust our competitors. They are only after your money (whereas we REALLY DO CARE™).

How to Find Yourself

proclaim:

"I'm the Best Me I Can Be"

"Believe who you are, with a capital BE!"

"My inner child is a brat."

"I I I I I I I I I I I I I I I I I I I I I I I I I I I I I I I I – that's who I am."

We have belts two sizes too small for the uptight who are comfortable being that way.

We have wage slaves someplace in Asian cellars where it's really sweaty and we don't tell anyone about who turn out custom-made, ultra-tight, circulation-stopping underwear made from thorny material for our masochistic personalities.[25]

So now you can see how hard we strive to serve ALL tastes in the Who Am I industry.

We down here at "Buy You" believe nothing is shameful when it comes to flouting your innermost being in the most public places.

We say, Take pride. We say, Take your checkbook to the nearest "Buy You" outlet, and splurge.

Go ahead, treat yourself to another you.

As we say down here at "Buy You," *Be the best you your money can buy.*

---

[25] And you'd be really surprised if you knew how many of these particular articles we sold each year.

The First Annual Convention of Madmen and Weird People

An Eye Witness Report

Opening Ceremonies

A journal I was freelancing for had heard about "something strange" going on over at the City Convention Center and suggested I go over and have a look. Maybe write something up for either the leisure or business sections, depending on what this convention was really all about.

Entering the hall I moved toward the dais. I passed circles of huddled, loose-limbed folks. The convention opened with the striking of the gavel. Unfortunately, the guy up on the dais struck the gavel on his own head. Repeatedly. Until he knocked himself out. Pandemonium broke out. The order of business was postponed until later.

Later, the second attempt at opening ceremonies followed pretty closely that of the first attempt, except someone had thought it prudent to confiscate the gavel. The same official on the dais improvised by rapping his head on the dais–repeatedly–and the convention was called to order.

"Old business?"

As this was the First Annual Convention of Madmen and Weird People, the issue of old business was only lingered upon for an hour and a half in stunned silence, as nobody knew what to do.

"New business?"

A small, intense man in his fifties wearing a grizzled sweater and a blue Mohawk hairdo leapt up to make a motion.

"I move we repeal the law of gravity!"

The motion was seconded and passed, although nobody floated away.

I turned my attention to a particularly deranged-looking man sitting next to me—he wore bright purple clothes and held two shiny marbles against his nostrils, and muttered over and over to himself, "She sells sea shells by the sea shore, but does she make any money?" I interrupted him, inquiring as to whether he was a certified madman or merely a weird person. He ceased his mumbling to stare at me warily for a few moments. He removed the marbles from his nostrils and glanced about. He leaned toward me to whisper out the side of his mouth.

"Fifteen years this January I've been round the bend and never had the urge to look back. I've found when you're nuts, you're cared for. Competent people see to it that you're feeling well, and regular folks are terrified. It's what I looked for in business and in money, and all the time it was waiting for me in insanity. Are you out of your mind, too?"

I told him I was an impartial observer doing a journalistic study. He immediately went pale and grew anxious.

"Hey, don't you give me away. I got a good thing going. Nice meeting you." With that, he shoved the two marbles back against his nostrils and began muttering, "Peter Piper picked a peck of

(or a reasonable facsimile)

pickled peppers, so he was probably a pretty weird guy, too."

Meanwhile, a ruckus had kicked up back on the dais. The Sergeant-at-Arms and the Treasurer were having a very vocal discussion about the merits of having five minutes of silent eye rolling and gnashing of teeth in honor of uncertified mad people everywhere. The Sergeant-at-Arms thought it would be, "… a useless gesture and that half-baked loonies in foreign countries were not worth the time, let alone the effort …" Yet the Treasurer was persuaded that "… mentally defective people the world over should band together and be supportive no matter the degree of dementia …" The audience cheered both simultaneously and rose to their feet to sing any song that popped into their heads in different keys and tempos.

Everyone laughed and appeared to be a having a fine old time.

I was not overly alarmed by the skewed proceedings, having been assured by the organizers that the gathering was taking place under close medical supervision. I located one of the physicians responsible, and asked about his motivations in sponsoring such a peculiar event.

"After much discussion, we thought it would be good therapy if a lot of crazy people got together in a supportive atmosphere where essentially they run the show and hence may experience a sense of responsibility and accomplishment which would lend itself to a more positive self-image." He winked. "Though some of the things they think up are pretty way out."

One of the way-out things they thought up was nakedness. It was never pinpointed who began the stampede toward *au natural* but it was believed to have commenced in the northwest corner of the auditorium where an impromptu zipper symphony was taking place. A zipper symphony, it should be explained, is what occurs when people with several different lengths of zipper on their pants, skirts, jackets, and/or boots come together to make music but are unable to play any instrument or carry a tune; so they resort to zipping and unzipping their garments in high, sharp tones but with plenty of rhythm. It appears that in this case someone had hit a low, flat note and then forgot to zip up. The garment slipped from the hips and fell to the ground. By-standers thought this a very good idea. Soon many madmen and weird women divested themselves of their garments. There was much tossing of fabric into the air accompanied by whoops of celebration. People hugged one another. There was little or no sexual activity reported, for the vast majority of the weird people had forgotten all about their reproductive urges. They just rubbed their bodies with buttered popcorn and left over cigarette stubs and made do.

The rent-a-cop brigade was summoned and order restored.

The main order of business from the dais dealt primarily with fashioning a charter. Many suggestions were made from the floor, the majority of which were rejected as not making any sense whatsoever. But in the end, a charter was created and overwhelmingly approved. The complete document is included below.

United charter for certified madmen and weird people

1. We weirdoes are uniformly combined and amassed to speak out passionately on burning issues of the day and leave the cooler ones till the end of the month.
2. We hereby do state unequivocally and with due urgency that to insure the honorable continuance of the race (i.e. mad humans and weird types) a special fund be set up to investigate why so many of us have forgotten about sex and, once we remember, to perfect mad ejaculation and weird insemination.

(or a reasonable facsimile)

3. It is also duly noted that we all like soft, furry animals but that this is not an imperative, just a really good feeling.
4. Also, we wish to institute a Commission of Borderline Cases to figure out which way is up, which way is down, and whether or not there really is a sideways, or is this just something sane people made up to keep us idiots confused?
5. Before we forget, we hereby declare and do state in whichever order comes first, that night shall follow day, and day shall follow night, and that this state of affairs will remain so until somebody comes up with a better idea.
6. That Bertha Smiles, a fat lady from Omaha, should stop spitting a fine film of moisture across your face when she talks to you and save it for group therapy where such behavior is warranted and accepted, nay, even looked forward to.

ARTICLE I. We should do this more often.
ARTICLE II. Very similar to Article I, but with a few minor modifications.
ARTICLE III. Each mad person retains his, hers, or its sovereignty; each weird person retains his, hers or its independence; everyone else may have what's left.
ARTICLE IV. In determining questions at next year's convention, everyone shall have at least one vote, except A. Z. Nutswell because of the zipper incident. (This may be repealed or lightly modified by one percent of the vote when tempers cool down.)
ARTICLE V. That if anyone present becomes sane or even somewhat conventional within the intervening year, he, she or it can no longer attend future conventions without written permission and/or much regret.

How to Find Yourself

ARTICLE VI. Of no importance, so we'll leave this one out.
ARTICLE VII. As we are beginning to lose count of these articles, so we'll stop here and begin over again next time.
Signed by the Committee for Mad People:

‡´∞à═══*$ }}}}*　　　　　　　　　#¶∞{{ ^
　　OO　 = mmm ¿~j~+!　　　　 «
&=&∞∞!!&&&　　　　　　 whee!
　XpXxXX X　　　　　　　　　　　 èé　　　x

　　　　　　　x**‡　　¶0!∞

Closing Ceremonies
As time was pressing in and evening coming on, more and more attendees were beginning to drool for a warm bed while others patted their individual tummies and murmured, "Home sweet home."

The closing ceremonies were poignant and brief. The Secretary General, the Sergeant-at-Arms, and Treasurer made three speeches simultaneously.

The Secretary General shouted, "Vote for me. If elected, I will serve. But I'll only serve if I'm accompanied by a side order of fries and fresh farm eggs over easy."

The Sergeant-at-Arms bragged, "I'm tougher than all of you put together. I don't care if I wet my pants and call it 'something funny happening down there', I'm strong. Feel my lip."

The treasurer said, "Dues. Who hasn't paid their dues? We have to pay our due. The dues are due. Due dues. Due dues. Due dues. Due dues."

With tears streaming down their faces in heartfelt sentiment, everyone said as one voice, "Goodbye, goodbye, goodbye," over and over again, waving meekly.

The crowd dispersed, shuffling away in a melancholy but

(or a reasonable facsimile)

satisfied spirit.

Coming out of the Convention Hall and into the fading evening light, and breathing in the fresh air, I thought, "How strange it all is." Beyond that, I didn't really want to think about it any more.

Further Reading

Your Friend, the Navel, Dr. Dexter Putty. Lowroad Publications, New York

Who Am I, Who Are You, Who Are They, Who Are We, Who's She, Who's He, Is That You? a study in mass confusion, by the members of a madhouse just down the road in Portland, Maine. Nuts-in-May Publishers, also just down the road, but in a different city in a different state.

People I Have Met, Roger Doger. Bankrupt Press, Ltd.

People I Haven't Met, ibid.

People I'd Like to Meet, burp.

Bad Thighs, the autobiography of a sexual maniac, with illustrations, John Doe III. Weird Books, Nebraska.

Yes I Can, No You Wont, one hundred and one schizophrenic case histories.

Autobiography, Anonymous. The Far Away Press.

How to Find Yourself

The Dirty Places on Your Body: What they could mean to you, how to use them to the best advantage, Anonymous (again, but this time we don't blame him.)

How to Die, the unavoidable made palatable, Henri-Jean du Doughé, the famous French chef. Pastry Publications, Somewhere, France

Death and You!, a self-help book on how to get the most out of a once-in-a-lifetime experience, Honey Bess Sue. Sometimes Books, Florida

ME, ME, ME, ME, ME, ME, ME, ME, ME, ME, ME, a study in self-absorption, Mrs. Mildred Flat and Mr. Harvey Round. Reprint Publications

Oh!, the first part of a trilogy on Selfhood.

Ah!, the second part of the trilogy.

Ee!, the third part.

Huh?, the condensed version.

Glossary

Self
1) Who you are; 2) Who you think you are; 3) Who you might be; 4) Somebody else; 5) All of the above.

Doubt
An odd feeling that something's not right.

Self-doubt
A very odd feeling that something's not right.

Soul
Mythical object; first mentioned by the sixteenth-century Russian sheep farmer, Soulovich, in his memoirs, Soul, Lamb Cutlets, and Me, and ever since has regularly regained the cultural spotlight as an enviable, though elusive object to possess.

Inner being
Something way, way deep down, with only a little bit peeking out where people can see it.

Depression
An organic chain reaction that is sometimes known to backfire.

Navel
See Center of the universe.

Center of the universe
See Navel.

Onanism
Regressive fun. Not to be mistaken for a true sense of self.

Suicide
Opposite of Life, although there has been no foolproof confirmation on this.

Signey Heller
The first person known to have discovered himself and not suffered from adverse side effects. Originator of the phrase, "Oh Wow!" Died circa 1900, although some people maintain he's just faking it and wants attention.

Madness
Look it up in the dictionary.

Sanity
Look in the mirror; on second thought, don't.

Tony Smiles
The first person to cast doubt on the value of knowing yourself; maintained it was a figment of the imagination; claimed he'd proven it by writing numerous papers on the subject, then dropping them in the mailbox but forgot to put postage on the envelope. Disappeared mysteriously one day.

Francis Grinning
Claims Tony Smiles was a figment of her imagination, and that she forgot about him one day, which at least explains his mysterious disappearance.

Life
A burden, although the alternative does not have a large, influential band of supporters.

Aesthetics
A word with vaguely feminine properties; macho men usually shun pronouncing it; homosexuals can become fixated; everyone else couldn't care less.

Christianity
Originally had something to do with Christ, now much abused.

Lutherans
I'd rather not get into all this.

Jews
Listen, as this is a nonsectarian book, these subjects will be avoided.

An avoided subject
An embarrassment, such as the current President of the United States, or this book.

This book
See The end

The end
An inevitability, and yet, in a way, a relief.

Endnote

This has been a book about how to find yourself. What to do with yourself, once found, is not within this book's province (although a companion volume *could* be in preparation if the present volume sells really, really well; working title: "I'm Me: Now What?").

Acknowledgments

The author would like to thank all the imaginary people in this book who gave of their time, and whose permission to be quoted extensively is gratefully acknowledged.

About the Author

Vincent Eaton and everyone else in this book are one and the same person, although we're not too sure about a couple of people.

The Back of the Book